Evidence and Paul's Journeys

Evidence and Paul's Journeys

An Historical Investigation
into the Travels of the Apostle Paul

Jefferson White

Parsagard Press

Parsagard Press

2586 Hickory Mill
Hilliard, OH 43026

Manufactured in the United States of America

Cover Design by Jefferson White

Cover Art: *The situation of the ship on the fifteenth morning,* painted by H. Smartly, engraved by H. Adlard. From James Smith, *The Voyage and Shipwreck of St. Paul* (1880 edition), page 140.

Unless otherwise noted, all scripture references are from the New International Version

Many thanks to PFR for editorial assistance.

Publisher's Cataloging-in-Publication
(Provided by Quality Books, Inc.)

White, Jefferson, 1950-
  Evidence and Paul's journeys : an historical
investigation into the travels of the apostle Paul /
Jefferson White. -- 1st ed.
  p. cm.
  Includes bibliographical references and index.
  LCCN: 00-108934
  ISBN: 0-9705695-0-5

  1. Paul, the Apostle, Saint,--Journeys--Mediterranean
Region. 2. Apostles--Biography. 3. Church history--
Primitive and early church, ca. 30-600. 4. Bible. N.T.
Acts--Criticism, interpretation, etc. 5. Mediterranean
Region--Description and travel. I. Title.

BS2506.W45 2001   225.9'2
                                    QBI00-970

For My Parents

Contents

Prologue

The Problem of Evidence

The gospel teaches that no one can know God without faith in Christ. It is thus faith, and not evidential demonstration, that lies at the heart of Christianity.

At the same time, the New Testament claims to be historically true. Other religions may rest on spiritual truths that are divorced from any historical context or claim, but faith in Jesus rests upon the truth of the events narrated in the New Testament. Faith in Christ is inseparable from the belief that certain events occurred and that the record of those events is true. The life of Jesus is more than just a spiritual event, it is an event in history. Thus Christians are faced with the problem of evidence.

Because the New Testament was written almost two thousand years ago, the amount of evidence that has come down to us is necessarily limited. Just a few fragmentary pagan and Jewish sources from the first century directly attest to the existence of Jesus and of the early church. On the other hand, there is a large amount of indirect, or collateral, evidence. The New Testament records hundreds of details that are confirmed by independent historical sources. This massive body of evidence is cumulatively impressive, though it is not easily summarized.

According to the book of Acts, the Apostle Paul traveled in the eastern Roman empire for more than a dozen years, preaching and teaching. Luke, whom tradition names as the author of Acts, provides us with a complex and detailed narrative of those journeys. Luke tells us about local political boundaries and titles. He describes the social characteristics of cities and provinces. He tells us about the distances traveled on land and on sea, and reveals how long it took to cover those distances. He describes Paul's arrests and trials, and details legal maneuverings in different jurisdictions. He tells of Paul's dealings with individuals who also appear in pagan and Jewish historical sources.

Indeed, Luke is astonishingly accurate when recording the political, social, and legal details of the cities and provinces of the eastern Roman empire. His accuracy becomes even more impressive when we discover that many of those details were true only in the middle decades of the first century, the era of Paul's travels.

There are a few spectacular confirmations of Luke's narrative. His account of Paul's shipwreck, for example, is dramatically confirmed in detail by meteorological and nautical evidence. This evidence decisively demonstrates that Paul's shipwreck must have occurred just as Luke records it, that it could not have happened any other way. But this kind of demonstration is rare. What we generally possess are many small pieces of evidence that add up to a coherent whole. It is the evidence as a whole that demonstrates the extraordinary historical accuracy of Luke's narrative.

However, before we turn to the evidence, there is a theoretical question that must be addressed. What exactly is *evidence*?

The answer to this question is not as simple as one might think. In the academic world, biblical scholars are dramatically divided on the question of the historical truth of the New Testament. First, there are the radical scholars, who argue that the New Testament is largely myth. Second, there are the liberal scholars, who argue that the New Testament is a mixture of history and myth, then disagree among themselves over which is which. Third, there are the conservative scholars, who argue that the New Testament is largely, or wholly, true history.

It is important to understand that the fundamental disagreement among these scholars has nothing to do with the evidence as such. Rather, their disagreement is over the *definition* of what constitutes evidence. Radical and liberal scholars begin with the assumption that philosophical theory trumps empirical evidence. In their view, if a scholar possesses the proper academic credentials and has created a complex theory about a biblical passage that is highly regarded by other scholars, then this theory is in *itself* evidence that decides the question of the historical truth of that passage.

Take, for example, the account of Paul's shipwreck. Early in the nineteenth century, liberal scholars argued that the Acts narrative of that shipwreck was a literary fantasy written to glorify Paul. Following the discovery of the meteorological and nautical evidence that pointed to the accuracy of Luke's account, this view shifted. Scholars then argued that the account of the shipwreck was accurate, but that Luke stole it from some other historical source and rewrote it to cast Paul as the hero. You will note that, in both cases, the argument that was made was not based on any real evidence, but upon a theory about the nature of the text.[1] What matters to radical and liberal scholars is the tailoring of empirical evidence to fit a theoretical position, and not the evidence itself.

Eta Linnemann, a leading radical scholar, put the matter this way in 1989, shortly after repudiating her life's work:

> "...the underlying historical-critical approach [of liberal and radical scholarship] is a series of pre-judgments which are not themselves the result of scientific investigation. They are rather dogmatic premises, statements of faith, whose foundation is the absolutizing of human reason as a controlling apparatus."[2]

For the reader who is interested in these "Scholar Wars" (which is probably never going to be the title of a major motion picture) W.W. Gasque's book, *A History of the Interpretation of the Acts of the Apostles,* is a good place to begin one's education. Although a bit heavy-going for the general reader, this study lays bare the major issues in the scholarly divide over the historical truth of the book of Acts.

Because the present book is concerned with an analysis of empirical evidence, rather than with scholarly theory, we will not be dealing with those issues here. Still, we require a theory of evidence in order to know what evidence to include or exclude in our argument. The evidential theory of this study can be expressed in two rules:

1) The biblical record is assumed to be true unless it can be shown to be false.
2) If a contradiction is alleged to exist between the biblical record and other historical evidence, and there is a reasonable explanation to account for it, the contradiction is not proved.

By the use of these two principles alone, most of radical and liberal biblical scholarship is rendered irrelevant in any rational analysis of the historical evidence. Those readers who prefer theoretical argument to empirical proof have picked up the wrong book.

The present study is also an attempt to do something new under the sun. Most books written for the general reader on the subject of biblical evidence tend to be superficial in their examination of that evidence. Even the best of such studies barely scratch the surface. In part, this is due to an assumption that the evidence is too technical, or too involved, for the average reader to follow. In part it is due to a bias that regards scholarly specialists as being the only people who can properly understand and weigh the evidence. Neither of these propositions is true.

It needs to be understood that modern biblical scholarship, even of the conservative variety, is inherently subversive of any attempt to understand the evidence as such. The tendency of biblical scholars is to value erudition over truth. They wish to understand the problematic, rather than the probable. This is why scholars are often less capable of weighing evidence than are non-scholars.

The use of biblical scholarship in the writing of this book is analogous to the employment of expert witnesses in a court of law. At trial, experts are only allowed to testify according to the legal rules of evidence, and not according to the – often subjective – standards of their profession.

The two rules listed above govern the analysis of evidence in this book. Although this study rests on the work of biblical scholars, it is most emphatically not a work of biblical scholarship. In these pages, the New Testament's claim of historical truth is the sole question under consideration. The purpose of this book is not to explain the biblical text or to narrate interesting historical facts. The purpose of this book is to provide an in-depth summary of the relationship of evidence to the record of Paul's journeys.

External Evidence

Chapter 1

The First Journey (47- 49 AD)

The narrative of Paul's journeys begins in the thirteenth chapter of Acts. Paul has been a Christian for fourteen years and now lives in Antioch, Syria. For several years, he has been one of the leaders of the mixed Jewish-gentile church there. Up to this point, the book of Acts has touched only briefly on Paul's career, but now he becomes the central figure of the narrative.

Sailing to Cyprus (Acts 13.1-.5)

According to Acts, Paul and Barnabas leave Antioch by way of its harbor at Seleucia, then land at Salamis on the island of Cyprus.

In the winter, it is impossible to sail in the Mediterranean. In the summer and fall the prevailing winds are from the West, and ships sailing from the Syrian coast can only land in the northern harbors of Cyprus. It is only in the spring that a ship can sail from Seleucia directly to Salamis.[1]

The Proconsul of Cyprus (Acts 13.6-.12)

After preaching in Salamis, Paul and Barnabas make their way across Cyprus to the capital at Paphos. They are invited to speak before the Roman Proconsul, Sergius Paulus. After addressing him and his court, they are challenged by a member of that court, a Jewish magician named Elymas.

The practice of magic was forbidden to the Jews by Jewish religious law. However, historical evidence reveals that Jewish magicians played a leading role in first century pagan society. Non-Jewish magicians even masqueraded as Jews, while Hebrew words were commonly used in the casting of spells.

According to the Jewish historian Josephus, a famous Jewish magician from Cyprus took part in the political intrigues of the Roman governor of Judea just a few years after the incident recorded in Acts. Is this the same individual who challenged Paul and Barnabas?

Unfortunately, Josephus states that the magician's name was Atomos, not Elymas. Most ancient magicians employed more than one alias, so it is possible that this could be the same individual. However, because the names are different, a positive identification cannot be established.

Luke says that the magician's name was also Bar-Jesus, and that this was a translation of "Elymas," a word meaning "wise" or "learned." The difficulty is that the name Bar-Jesus cannot possibly be translated as "Elymas." Some scholars have suggested that Luke is actually suggesting that "Elymas" is a translation of the word magician. While it is possible to read Luke's Greek in this manner, the most natural interpretation is that he is referring to the name Bar-Jesus.

But even if we assume that the author of Acts has made a linguistic mistake in equating "Elymas" with Bar-Jesus, this is the kind of mistake that we might expect Luke to make. He is the only New Testament writer who is not a Jew. Paul states (in Colossians

4.10-.14) that Luke is a gentile, and in Acts 1.19 Luke refers to Aramaic, the language of first century Palestinian Jews, as being "their" language. If Luke has mistranslated a Semitic name, this is an error that might be expected from a Greek-speaking gentile.[2]

As for the Proconsul Sergius Paulus, the historical evidence for this individual is intriguing. We know that the island of Cyprus was a Senatorial province during this era, so its governor was indeed a Proconsul. And there is a "Lucius Sergius Paulus" who is listed in Roman records as Curator of the Tiber just a few years before Paul and Barnabas visited Cyprus. Because service as Curator in the Roman system was often followed by an appointment to a Proconsulship, this may be the man named in Acts. Unfortunately, Acts does not reveal Sergius Paulus' first name, so once again a positive identification cannot be made.[3]

The Journey to Pisidian Antioch (Acts 13.13-.48)

From Cyprus, Paul and Barnabas sail to Perga in the province of Pamphylia. They travel by road northward to Pisidian Antioch, where they are invited to speak in the Jewish synagogue.

Luke's geography is correct. Perga was on the southern coast of what is today Turkey. Pisidian Antioch was located higher up in the interior, linked to Perga by a major road. We know from inscriptions found in the ruins of this city that a colony of Jews lived there during the first century, so there was probably a synagogue.[4] The technical Greek term that Luke uses to describe the officials of the synagogue, *Archisynagogi*, is correct.[5]

Women in Pisidian Antioch (Acts 13.50)

Following Paul's speech at the synagogue, a number of Jews and gentiles become Christians. The opponents of Paul and Barnabas then organize the leading women and men of the city against them, and force them to leave.

In the first century, women were generally prohibited from taking part in public life. The province of Galatia, where Pisidian Antioch was located, was one of a few Roman provinces where women were active in public affairs. Acts also records public participation by women when Paul visited the provinces of Macedonia and Asia. Historical evidence reveals that these were the only other provinces in which Paul traveled where women were allowed to take part in public life. The Acts narrative is confirmed on this social detail.[6]

Iconium and Lycaonia (Acts 14.1-.6)

From Pisidian Antioch, Paul and Barnabas travel to Iconium to preach, and soon run into trouble. Their local Jewish and pagan opponents, together with the city authorities, plan to start a riot. Hearing of the conspiracy, Paul and Barnabas flee into Lycaonia, to the cities of Lystra and Derbe, and to the surrounding region.

According to secular history, the magistrates of Alexandria, Egypt, played a role in the anti-Jewish riots that swept that city during this era. There are other first century instances when city officials encouraged riots. The fact that the magistrates of Iconium conspired in organizing a riot fits the times.[7]

Acts reports that Paul and Barnabas "fled into Lycaonia, to the cities of Lystra and Derbe, and to the surrounding region." There are several pieces of evidence that illuminate this passage. First, when Luke speaks of the surrounding region he is probably referring to the *regio* defined by Roman political boundaries. In 37 AD, ten years before Paul and Barnabas' arrival, Rome took control of the part of Lycaonia containing Lystra and Derbe. In 72 AD, Rome took over eastern Lycaonia and united the whole area under Roman rule.

Acts refers to just two cities as being in this region, Lystra and Derbe. Laranda, which was a much larger city than either of these, was located during this era in non-Roman Lycaonia. Thus Luke's omission of Laranda, the largest city in the *geographical* area, reflects the *political* boundaries of the middle of the first century.

There is additional evidence on this matter. Acts states that Paul and Barnabas fled from Iconium into "the region of Lycaonia." The city of Iconium is also geographically part of Lycaonia. However, the people living in Iconium were ethnic Phrygians. In the first century, the Romans generally organized regions according to ethnicity. It was only in the later empire that they reorganized political boundaries along strictly geographical lines. And in the later empire, Iconium was part of the region of Lycaonia. Luke's narrative, which separates Iconium from Lycaonia, belongs to the earlier period of Roman history.

Some scholars argue that it cannot be established with certainty that Iconium lay outside Lycaonia in the first century, and point to first century pagan writers who seem to disagree on this question. However, of the writers known to have actually visited Lycaonia, all state the matter as Luke does. When referring to Iconium as part of Lycaonia, in every case they are speaking of geographical, and not political, boundaries. When they refer to Iconium as being part of the region of Phrygia, they are speaking in political or ethnic terms. It is only among writers who have not visited the area that these identifications become confused. Thus Luke's assertion is confirmed by the preponderance of the historical evidence.[8]

Lystra (Acts 14.8-.18)

In the city of Lystra, Paul heals a man. This causes a riot, during which the people shout in their native dialect that Paul and Barnabas are gods come to earth. They call Barnabas Zeus and Paul Hermes.

In the original Greek, Acts states that Lystran cripple had the faith to be "saved," the word in this context meaning "healed." The word is not used in the Christian sense, but follows pagan usage in referring to a physical, rather than a spiritual, salvation. No

Christian in the second century, or later, would have used the word "saved" in this fashion. By that time, the church was locked in mortal combat with paganism and pagan ideas. To later Christians, the word saved had only meaning – eternal salvation. This piece of linguistic evidence demonstrates that this passage in Acts was written during the first century.[9]

Concerning the crowd's Lycaonian dialect, historical evidence reveals that the lower classes of the interior of Asia Minor still spoke in their native tongues as late as the first century. This was in contrast to the more heavily populated areas along the Mediterranean coast, where native languages had largely disappeared in favor of Greek. Thus Luke's reference to a native dialect in this inland city is accurate.[10]

It is interesting that the crowd called Barnabas Zeus and Paul Hermes. The populace of every locality in the ancient world worshipped deities that were considered to be the patrons of their area. Archeological evidence reveals that the Zeus-Hermes combination was the local cult of the city of Lystra. A number of inscriptions have been discovered that are dedications to the two gods, linked in a common worship. The Roman poet Ovid, writing in the first century, portrays, in his poem "Metamorphoses," an appearance of these two gods to an old couple living not far from Lystra.

Nor is it particularly unusual that the local population of Lystra should want to worship Paul and Barnabas as gods. When Apollonius of Tyana, a pagan miracle worker, was tried before the Emperor Domitian at the end of the first century, one of the charges against him was that he had allowed himself to be worshipped as a god. The Greek writer Lucian also tells of an incident, occurring early in the first century, when a provincial town worshipped a wonder worker as a god.

Paul is the central figure in Acts, so it may seem strange that the people of Lystra identified Barnabas as Zeus, who was the more important of the two gods. Luke does not tell us why this identification was made. However, historical evidence reveals that it was a common belief in the ancient world that when two gods came to earth, the lesser one did the talking. Since Paul did the preaching, the people probably concluded that Barnabas must be the greater god. This is a small historical point, but it underscores the authenticity of the narrative.[11]

The Controversy over the Gentile Christians (Acts 15)

Paul and Barnabas return to Antioch, bringing the first missionary journey to a close. Following their return, a theological controversy arises in the Antioch church. Jewish Christians, arriving from Judea, teach that gentiles cannot become Christians without being circumcised according to Jewish religious law.

To settle the matter, the church sends Paul and Barnabas to Jerusalem to meet with the Apostles. The fifteenth chapter of Acts records the events of this important meeting. The leadership of the Jerusalem church, which includes both Peter and James, concludes the meeting by stating that gentile converts do not have to become Jews.

The historical existence of James, the brother of Christ, as well as his position as a leader in the church at Jerusalem, is confirmed by the first century Jewish historian Josephus. Josephus states that when Festus, the Roman Procurator of Judea, suddenly died (about 61 AD), the Jewish High Priest Ananus decided to take advantage of the temporary lapse of Roman authority to call the Sanhedrin into session. He then "brought before them the brother of Jesus, who is called Christ, whose name was James, and some others, and when he had formed an accusation against them as breakers of the law, he delivered them to be stoned..."

James' death is not recorded in the New Testament. The Acts narrative ends more than a year before the stoning of James. Thus Josephus' statement not only confirms the existence of James and the role he played in the Jerusalem church, it provides us with additional historical details about him.[12]

James' Speech (Acts 15.17-.18)

During his speech, James quotes from the Greek version of the Old Testament, called the Septuagint. Some historians have argued that a first century Judean Jew would never have used the Septuagint to make a theological argument. They also point out that James' theological argument cannot even be made if the standard Hebrew text is used, since it differs dramatically from the Septuagint.

However, first century Jewish practices of biblical interpretation, and their use of the Septuagint, are historical matters that are very far from being settled. Other historians have argued that James' scriptural proof is precisely the kind of argument that we can expect from that time and place.

Two other points should be kept in mind. First, the New Testament contains a letter written by James, and this letter uses the Septuagint exclusively when quoting the Old Testament. Second, Luke is obviously summarizing James' speech in Acts and is not reporting it. Luke also consistently uses the Septuagint when quoting the Old Testament. He may have used it here to reconstruct James' speech, whichever version of the scriptures James actually used on this occasion.[13]

The Apostolic Decree (Acts 15.22-.29)

The meeting in Jerusalem ends with the Apostles and elders deciding that gentiles do not have to become Jews in order to become Christians. However, they set down a list of prohibitions that are directly related to Jewish religious law. "Eat no food that has been offered to idols; eat no blood; eat no animal that has been strangled; and keep yourselves from immorality."

Except for the warning against immorality, the prohibitions were designed to keep Christians from ritual uncleanness as defined by Jewish religious law. There is considerable evidence, from the second century, that some gentile churches were still following this list of prohibitions. However, by that time, the decisive break with Judaism had occurred and Christianity was no longer Jewish in either practice or orientation. Most churches were no longer following these prohibitions. The fact that some churches still followed these rules demonstrates a continuing adherence to the earlier tradition.[14]

Chapter 2

The Second Journey (49-52 AD)

Timothy's Parents and Friends (Acts 16.1-.5)

The second missionary journey begins with Paul revisiting the cities of the first journey. In Lystra, Paul takes on a new assistant, Timothy, whose mother was a Jew, but whose father was a gentile.

Historical evidence reveals that Jewish-pagan intermarriage was comparatively rare in the first century. Jews were highly conscious of being a people set apart and seldom married gentiles. However, there were areas in the Roman empire where Jews had long been settled in isolation from the larger Jewish community. In these mainly inland, rural regions, they intermarried with the local population. First century grave inscriptions from Lystra reveal that Jewish-gentile intermarriage was common there.[1]

Luke records that Timothy was well spoken of by believers in Lystra and Iconium. This is an odd statement, since Acts usually refers to "Lystra and Derbe." Only in this passage does Acts refer to "Lystra and Iconium."

Archeological evidence clears up the mystery. Lystra was on the same trading route as Iconium and was located nearer to it than to Derbe. All of Lystra's commercial and social ties were with Iconium. Luke refers, in other passages, to "Lystra and Derbe" because they were the two main cities in the Roman *political* region of Lycaonia. But socially and geographically, it was Lystra and Iconium that were linked. Thus it makes sense that Timothy was known to the Christians at Lystra and Iconium, rather than to the Christians at Lystra and Derbe. Luke's narrative fits the local circumstances.[2]

Paul's Journey to Troas (Acts 16.6-.10)

Paul and his companions travel from Lystra and Derbe through the Phrygian region of Galatia. They then pass into the Roman province of Asia, and travel north until they reach the border of Mysia. Turning west, they journey to Troas, a city on the eastern shore of the Aegean Sea.

In these details, Luke follows the ancient overland routes across central and western Turkey, including the mountain tracks down to Troas and the Aegean. While the mountain tracks cannot now be traced with certainty, Luke accurately refers to each Roman administrative district by name.[3] The single exception is Mysia, which was the name of an ancient territory, and not a Roman district. Luke uses this place name to identify the point at which they turned west to go over the mountains to Troas.[4]

The Voyage From Troas to Philippi (Acts 16.11-.12)

From Troas, Paul and his company board a ship to sail across the Aegean Sea to Macedonia. The ship anchors for the night off the island of Samothrace, and lands the next day at Neapolis, harbor town of the city of Philippi.

Luke's account of the two-day sail from Troas to Philippi is accurate. Meteorological evidence demonstrates that it would take two days for them to reach Neapolis, given the time of year and the prevailing winds. Samothrace is a likely overnight stop. In a later passage (Acts 20.6), Luke records a trip in the opposite direction, this time from Philippi to Troas. On that occasion, he says that the voyage took five days. Meteorological evidence also confirms that statement, based on the time of year and the prevailing winds.[5]

In the twelfth verse, there is a question of whether Luke is saying that Philippi was a city of the First District of Macedonia, or whether he is stating that Philippi was the first, or leading, city of the district. Luke's Greek can be read either way. The Roman province of Macedonia was divided into four districts, which were numbered rather than named. Philippi was in the First District. It was also the leading city of the district, being a Roman colony. Luke's statement fits the historical circumstances in either case.[6]

The Lydian Woman (Acts 16.13-.14)

On the Sabbath day, Paul and his associates went out of the city gate of Philippi to the riverside, looking for the Jewish place of prayer. At the river, they met a woman from Thyratira, in Lydia, a dealer in purple fabrics. Though a gentile, she worshipped the God of the Jews. After listening to Paul, she became a Christian.

Modern translations of Acts sometimes state that the woman's name was Lydia. But Luke's Greek actually reads: "the Lydian woman." Thyratira, her city of origin, was located in the territory of the ancient kingdom of Lydia. Thyratira was famous as a center for the dyeing of fabric, so her occupation corresponds to the leading industry of that area. Luke's statement that the Lydian woman was "a seller of purple" means that she sold the most expensive line of fabric.

Once again, we see the social contrast between the different Roman provinces regarding the status of women. For this "seller of purple" was a businesswoman. This fits the social

circumstances, not only of her native Lydia in the Roman province
of Asia, but of the province of Macedonia where she was staying.
In most of the rest of the Roman empire, an independent
businesswoman would not have been welcome.

Luke states that the Lydian woman was a gentile who was a
follower of Judaism. Archeological diggings in Thyratira reveal
that a Jewish colony existed there in the first century. According to
inscriptional evidence, a large number of gentiles in Thyratira were
Jewish proselytes. Again, the historical evidence fits the local
circumstances described by Luke.[7]

The Arrest of Paul and Silas (Acts 16.16-.21)

*Paul and Silas are arrested in Philippi. They are charged with
disturbing the peace and with teaching customs that Roman
citizens are forbidden to follow.*

Philippi was a Roman colony, strategically planted by Rome to
control the surrounding area. It was originally settled by Roman
citizens. Prior to the first century, Roman law prohibited a citizen
from practicing a religious cult that was not authorized by the state.
By the middle of the first century, this law was honored largely in
the breach. The sheer number of eastern cults that had inundated
the empire placed the matter beyond the control of the Roman
government.

First century political authorities generally tolerated any cult
that was not involved in either politics or crime, though sometimes
a cult would be banned because of some other controversy. The
charge against Paul and Silas, that they were teaching religious
doctrines not permitted to Romans, fits the century before Christ
better than it does the middle of the first century. Because of this,
some scholars have questioned the historical accuracy of Luke's
statement.

Other scholars argue that the charge may reflect an edict that
had recently been promulgated by the Emperor Claudius. About
the time that Paul arrived in Phillipi, Claudius expelled the Jews

from the city of Rome. Because Christianity was viewed as a Jewish sect, Christians would have shared in any public animus against the Jews. Thus the charge against Paul and Silas may echo Claudius' edict.

There is also a second possibility. Colonies are often more conservative than the mother country, preserving social attitudes that have long been discarded back home. A half century before Paul's visit to Philippi, the city of Rome had not allowed the practice of non-Roman religions within its walls. Philippi, which had been founded ninety years before Paul's visit, may have preserved the older Roman tradition.

Against this view, some scholars argue that Roman colonies ceased to be Roman after the first generation. Since they were generally planted in the midst of large native populations, the surrounding peoples, over time, gradually filtered into the colony and turned the Roman inhabitants into a minority.

At the time of Paul's arrest, it is probably true that very few of the residents of Philippi were Roman citizens, though the charge against him implies that the city was composed of nothing but Romans. There is some historical evidence that suggests that the non-Roman inhabitants of a Roman colony had an intermediate status between that of citizen and ordinary provincial. The charge made against Paul and Silas may reflect this intermediate status, or it may have been made by individuals who were themselves Roman citizens. However, apart from this passage in Acts, there is no definitive evidence as to whether this charge could legally have been made in Philippi at this time.

The procedures by which Paul and Silas were arraigned by the local magistrates are the correct ones. Under Roman law, there was no public prosecutor. Private citizens always undertook the prosecution of a breach of law, bringing their accusations to the local magistrates. A trial was held and the magistrates would decide whether any laws were broken.[8]

Paul and Silas are Beaten (Acts 16.22-.23)

After the accusers make their case, and at the instigation of the mob attending the proceedings, the magistrates strip Paul and Silas of their clothing and hand them over to be beaten.

Under first century Roman law, the magistrates had no authority to strip and beat Paul and Silas before the conclusion of the trial. This passage reveals a social instability that was often found in first century society. More than one ancient writer reports instances of local officials ignoring the law while under the influence of mobs. The Roman writer Horace, in one of his satires, depicts a provincial Roman magistrate engaged in striking various poses before an angry crowd, immediately changing his views with each change in their mood. The condition of many city governments in the Roman empire during this period did not much differ from this comic portrayal.

This passage does present an historical problem of another kind. Under first century Roman law, it was a capital offense for a local magistrate to beat a Roman citizen. Had the magistrates known that Paul and Silas were Romans, they would never have treated them as they did. Acts records that Paul and Silas did not reveal their citizenship until the following morning, after spending the night in jail. Some scholars argue that it is unbelievable that Paul and Silas would have hidden their Roman citizenship, since by revealing it they could have avoided both a beating and a night in jail.

This is a persuasive argument. But there are two possible explanations for their refusal to reveal that they were Romans. First, Paul's consistent policy, demonstrated throughout Acts, was to avoid identify himself as a Roman unless forced to do so. Paul lived in an era when Roman citizenship was rare. Anyone who was a Roman was politically and socially a class above everyone else. In both Acts and in his letters, Paul consistently presents himself as a Jew and as a preacher of the gospel, and not as a Roman. Acts reveals that his citizenship was a family inheritance. Few Jews in the first century were Romans, and most Jews had no use for the Romans. For Paul, the fact that he was a Roman citizen was a complicating factor in his ministry.

Second, it is also possible that the swift violence of events kept Paul and Silas from making a declaration of citizenship. With events out of control, they may have decided to wait until things cooled down.[9]

The Earthquake (Acts 16.23-.34)

Following their beating, Paul and Silas are put in prison for the night. About midnight, an earthquake occurs which badly damages the jail and frees the prisoners from their bonds. The awakened jailer rushes to the prison to discover that the doors are open. Thinking that the prisoners have escaped, he prepares to commit suicide. Paul sees him and calls out that all the prisoners are still there. The jailer brings Paul and Silas out of the jail, then he and his family are baptized. Paul and Silas spend the rest of the night as guests at his house.

The historical authenticity of this passage has often been questioned. First, the idea that an earthquake would open the doors of the prison, while also breaking the prisoners' bonds, is thought to be too convenient to be true. On the other hand, earthquakes are common in that area to this day. Nor is it inherently unlikely that doors would become unhinged, or that chains would come loose from walls, during an earthquake.

Second, there is the question as to how Paul knew, in the darkness, that the other prisoners were still in the prison. However, it is possible that the prisoners were placed together in an inner containment cell for the night. Archeological evidence, together with ancient literary evidence, reveals that Roman prisons often contained an inner cell large enough to hold a number of prisoners in strict confinement. Acts states that Paul and Silas were put in an inner cell, but does not say where the other prisoners were kept. They could have been in the inner cell with Paul and Silas.

Third, it has been argued that the jailer would not have tried to commit suicide without checking to see if his prisoners had really escaped. But we cannot now get inside the mind of the jailer. If the outer prison door was open, and he went in and found the inner door open as well, the logical conclusion would have been that the prisoners had escaped. Under Roman law, the jailer was responsible with his life for any prisoner entrusted to him. In Roman society, it was considered more honorable to commit suicide for betraying that kind of trust than to await execution.

Fourth, some scholars have argued that if Paul was able to see the jailer preparing to commit suicide, then the jailer should have been able to see Paul. But the jailer would have been looking into a dark cell from the outside. Paul, whose eyes would have been accustomed to the dark, could more easily see into the brighter outer chamber. The jailer may have been carrying a torch, though Luke does not say that.

Fifth, scholars have questioned whether Paul and Silas would have been permitted to spend the rest of the night as guests at the jailer's home. However, under Roman law, the jailer had only the responsibility to produce his prisoners when called upon to do so. Where or how he kept them in the meantime was up to him. The Philippian jailer must have known that the local magistrates would not react favorably to the fact that Paul and Silas had spent the night at his home, but he was apparently prepared to take that risk.

Taken as a whole, this passage in Acts reads like a popular tale and raises enough questions that some scholars doubt its historical authenticity. However, when taken point by point, there is nothing inherently improbable about any of the events contained in this account.[10]

The Magistrates Become Alarmed (Acts 16.35-.39)

The next morning, officers are sent by the magistrates to release Paul and Silas, with instructions to tell them to leave the city. When the officers arrive, Paul reveals that he and Silas are Roman citizens. He then tells them to bring the magistrates to him. The magistrates, in alarm, rush to the prison. They apologize for their actions, and beg Paul and Silas to leave the city.

First, there is the matter of the officers who are sent to the jail. Although it may seem strange to us today, most cities in the ancient Roman world had no policemen. Rome's legions were stationed on the frontiers of the empire, while auxiliary legions were placed in provinces that were politically unstable. Other than that, there were no police forces. Local law was maintained by local magistrates in league with citizens who acted as a vigilante force.

A few cities in the Roman empire were permitted to have what we would today call policemen. Roman colonies were permitted two such officials, called Lictors. Since Philippi was a Roman colony, Luke's reference to the officers who came to free Paul and Silas fits the local circumstances.[11]

Luke does not tell us why the magistrates thought that they could beat and jail Paul and Silas one day, then quietly ask them to leave town the next. Even putting aside the matter of Roman citizenship, the magistrates had no legal authority for publicly humiliating and beating them the previous day. Of course, that may be why they wanted Paul and Silas to leave. To bring them to trial now, with the case being subject to review by higher Roman authority, was not something the magistrates would have wanted to do. By simply ordering them out of the city, the magistrates were sweeping the matter under the rug.

It is at this point that Paul drops his bombshell. The result is electric. The magistrates come personally to the prison and beg them to leave. This response is a decisive piece of evidence that Acts belongs to the middle of the first century. In that era, a Roman citizen possessed an absolute exemption from being beaten or held in chains by a public authority. Only under extraordinary circumstances could such treatment be justified. In other words, the magistrates themselves faced criminal charges. In a similar incident, earlier in the century, the Emperor Augustus was forced to issue an edict to exempt a Roman official from severe punishment when that official sent an unruly citizen to Rome in chains.

However, by the end of the first century, the nature of Roman citizenship had changed dramatically. Beginning with the Emperor Claudius, citizenship began to be granted to ever larger numbers of people. It was no longer restricted to those whose ancestors had been Romans or who had performed some service to the Roman state. Instead, Roman citizenship became the property of almost anyone who wanted to pay for it.

As a result, citizenship became a worthless possession so far as guaranteeing one's civil rights was concerned. For example, Pliny, the Roman governor of Bithynia at the beginning of the second century, complains about the savage treatment of a Roman aristocrat who was brought to trial by the governor of a neighboring province. His indignation centers on the fact of the aristocrat's social status. Roman citizenship is not even mentioned. This was a radical change from Paul's day, and Luke's account reflects the earlier reality.[12]

In verse thirty-seven (and in another incident, recorded in Acts 22.25), Paul remarks that the magistrates could have beaten them legally had they been brought to trial. Some scholars dispute the accuracy of this statement. Before the first century, local magistrates had no power of corporal punishment against a Roman citizen. Beginning early in the first century, exceptions began to be made to this rule, since the geographical expansion of the empire made it inconvenient to send every citizen to Rome. By mid-century, Roman citizens could be beaten by provincial authorities after being convicted of a crime. However, this was allowed only for certain kinds of crimes and only if the citizen did not exercise his right of appeal to Rome.

We possess only a few records from the middle of the first century that refer to the provincial punishment of Roman citizens.

In each case, punishment was by the governor of the province and not by local authorities. Apart from Luke's testimony in Acts, there are no recorded incidents of local magistrates punishing Roman citizens. Of course, Philippi was a Roman colony, so the magistrates of that city would have been more likely to have that kind of power.[13]

It should be noted that, under first century Roman law, no local magistrate had the power to expel someone from a city. However, Acts does not state that the authorities were acting legally in their attempt to expel Paul and Silas. Their attempt to expel them has all the earmarks of illegal coercion.[14]

Thessalonica (Acts 17.1-.4)

Paul and Silas leave Philippi and pass through Amphipolis and Apollonia. On their arrival in Thessalonica, Paul goes directly to the Jewish synagogue to preach. Following his address, some of the Jews become Christians, as do some of the local gentile followers of Judaism – including some of the leading women of the city.

The route that Paul took from Philippi to Thessalonica was a major Roman highway, the Via Egnatia. The cities named by Luke were overnight stops on that route.[15]

The word used by Luke to denote the Gentiles in this passage is Hellenes (or Greeks). Though the city of Thessalonica was located in Macedonia, and not in Greece, Luke is not wrong. Historical evidence reveals that the first century inhabitants of Thessalonica regarded themselves as Greek.[16] The active social presence of women in this city should also be noted. This would not have been found in Greece itself.[17] In short, Luke accurately shows us a city that wants to be known as Greek, is located in Macedonia, and follows Macedonian social customs.

The Riot (Acts 17.5-.14)

At Thessalonica, a riot ensues. Because the mob is unable to find Paul and Silas, they drag Jason and several other local Christians before the magistrates. The magistrates compel Jason and the others to put up a bond against the continued presence of Paul and Silas in the city.

In the Greek, Luke calls the local magistrates Politarchs, which is an unusual title. However, archeologists have discovered numerous first century inscriptions in Thessalonica which reveal that this was in fact what the local magistrates were called.[18]
Thessalonica was a free, or self-governing, city. There were only a few such cities in the first century Roman empire. While Luke does not actually state that Thessalonica was self-governing, the city's status is indirectly revealed by him. Under first century Roman law, only the magistrates of a free city had the power to compel the kind of legal bond that Luke records as being required of Jason and the other Christians. Once again, Luke's account fits the local circumstances.[19]

Berea (Acts 17.10-.12)

Paul and Silas leave Thessalonica and travel to Berea. The leading women of the city are mentioned as being among those who became believers. Berea is in Macedonia.

Athens (Acts 17.13-.21)

Some of Paul's Jewish opponents from Thessalonica arrive in Berea. They stir up the population against him, so he decides to leave for Athens. Disturbed by the number of idols in that city, Paul goes each day to the Athenian marketplace to argue with anyone who will oblige him. He debates Epicurean and Stoic teachers, who bring him before the Areopagus Council to speak.

Historical evidence confirms that Athens was indeed a city of idols. The public marketplace in Athens, the Agora, was famous as a place of philosophical disputation. That Paul should go there and argue with the representatives of the leading philosophies of the time fits the local circumstances. Epicureanism and Stoicism were leading Greek philosophies until the end of the second century AD.[20]

The Areopagus Council was an ancient Athenian institution. In the century before Paul's visit, the Areopagus was a political body that regulated public manners and morals, as well as providing a forum to visiting lecturers. Inscriptional evidence from the first century indicates that the Council was still in existence, but the extent of its authority under Roman rule is unknown. From Luke's account, Paul's appearance before the Council does not appear to be coerced, nor does the Council seem to have any legal jurisdiction over him. It may be that the Areopagus had no political authority at this time and was simply a forum for debate.[21]

Paul's Speech Before the Areopagus (Acts 17.22-.31)

Paul begins his speech before the Areopagus by stating that he has seen with his own eyes that the Athenians are a very religious people. He points out that they possess a statue for every god and even a statue to the "unknown god." Paul then states that he has come to tell them who that unknown god is and that He is the only God. During his speech, Paul quotes two pagan poets.

Several non-Christian writers – Josephus, Pausanias, and Philostratus – write that the religiosity of the Athenian population was well known to the ancient world.[22] Writing in the middle of the second century, Pausanias also states that "In Athens there were altars to gods unknown." Early in the third century, Philostratus records that Athens is a place "where even unknown divinities have altars erected to them." [23]

As for Paul's quotes from two pagan poets, one is from a poem on astronomy by Aratus, who lived in the fourth century BC. Historical evidence reveals that this poem was popular in the first century. Since Aratus lived in the kingdom of Cilicia, the region where Paul grew to manhood, Paul would have had reason to know the work of this particular poet. [24]

Damaris (Acts 17.32-.34)

Among the few people who become believers in Athens, one woman is mentioned. Luke does not say that this woman was of high birth, as he does of women in other passages. Indeed, her name, Damaris, is an indication that she may have been a foreigner, since at the time this was not a Greek name. In the Athenian society of Paul's era, no respectable Greek woman would have been within earshot of Paul during his appearance before the Areopagus. [25]

Corinth (Acts 18.1-.2)

Paul leaves Athens and travels to Corinth, where he meets two Jews, Aquila and his wife Priscilla. Luke records that this couple had recently left Rome because the emperor had issued an edict expelling all Jews from the city.

The expulsion of the Jews by Claudius is recorded by three Roman historians: Suetonius, Dio Cassius, and Orosius. The date of this expulsion corresponds to the date of Paul's visit to Corinth, around 50 AD.

Suetonius writes that the Jews were expelled from Rome because of disturbances caused by someone named Chrestus. This passage is intriguing, since early pagan writers often confused the common name "Chrestus" with the Christian title "Christus" (the

Greek equivalent of the Jewish word "Messiah"). Suetonius obviously believes that Chrestus is the name of the individual who personally caused the disturbances within the Jewish community at Rome. What he may be reporting, however, is a controversy within the Jewish community over the question of whether Jesus was Messiah. If so, this passage would be the oldest surviving pagan reference to Christianity.[26]

Paul the Tentmaker (Acts 18.3)

Paul settles in Corinth for a time and pursues his trade of tent-making, along with Aquila and Priscilla who are also tent-makers.

An argument can be made that the Greek word, which is literally translated as "tent-maker," commonly referred to someone who was a leather worker. Paul's home province of Cilicia was known in the ancient world for its leather goods, so this would be a natural trade for Paul to follow.

It might seem strange that Paul, who was an educated man and who had been a rabbi, was also a leather worker. Educated men in antiquity, like educated men today, usually did not make their living with their hands. But from second century Jewish records, we know that it was the standard practice for a rabbi to support himself with a trade rather than to take money for being a religious teacher. This practice may have been followed in the first century, though there is no solid evidence on this matter. Acts itself provides no explanation as to why Paul was a leather worker.[27]

Paul's Corinthian Trial (Acts 18.5-.12)

Paul begins preaching full time in Corinth. He spends a year and a half in the city, preaching and teaching. Then some of his Jewish opponents hatch a conspiracy against him, bringing him before the Roman Proconsul, Gallio, for judgment.

Archeologists have discovered a first century inscription at Delphi, in central Greece, that contains a proclamation of the Emperor Claudius. The proclamation refers to Gallio as the Roman Proconsul of Greece in the year in which the proclamation was issued. That year corresponds to 52 AD, which is the approximate date of Paul's Corinthian trial. Proconsuls generally served for only one year.

This is the second independent chronological confirmation of the date of Paul's visit to Macedonia and Greece. The first was Claudius' edict expelling the Jews from Rome in 50 AD, which sent Aquila and Priscilla to Corinth. Then, a year and a half later, Paul is brought to trial before Gallio at the time of Gallio's Proconsulship in 52 AD. These are dramatic confirmations of Luke's historical accuracy.

A few scholars argue that someone writing Acts early in the second century could have discovered these dates in a secular source, and simply worked them into the text. But how likely is this? The answer is that it is extremely unlikely that someone writing later could have discovered this information.

First, the ancient world was simply not interested in doing historical research. Ancient writers would include historical details if those details were part of their immediate sources, but research in the modern sense was not done.

Second, there would have been few records for the writer to consult even if he had been interested in doing so. Indeed, most of the provinces of the Roman empire did not maintain permanent archives. Pliny, the Roman governor of Bithynia at the beginning of the second century, states in a letter that there existed no record of his predecessors in office, and Bithynia had been a Roman province for a hundred years. We know more of the details of Roman history today than did the ancient Romans.

Third, although Gallio's Proconsulship was undoubtedly recorded in the archives of Roman Senate, one would have had to have been a Roman of high rank to gain access to those archives.

Beginning in the sixties of the first century, no Christian would have been allowed in those archives, even one of high rank, since by that time being a believer in Christ was punishable by death.

Fourth, another way that a later Christian writer could have discovered the date of Gallio's Proconsulship was if his name had been on a locally minted coin. But we know a great deal about Roman coinage. The province of Greece never placed the names of its Proconsuls on coins during this period, while local Corinthian coins contain only the names of city magistrates.

Thus it is almost impossible that someone of a later generation could have discovered Gallio's name and date in some historical source and used that information in writing the book of Acts. The reference to Gallio's Proconsulship is either due to Luke's personal knowledge or is derived from his immediate sources. The same can be said about almost every other social and political fact that is found in the book of Acts. If a particular fact belongs to the middle of the first century, this is the same as saying that the writer of Acts, or his immediate sources, had personal knowledge of that fact.[28]

This is an important point. Since it is almost impossible that some later writer could have discovered this information on his own, Luke's account decisively points either to his own personal knowledge of that event or to the personal knowledge of his immediate sources. When Luke records that Gallio presided over Paul's trial in Corinth around 52 AD, it is because he has direct knowledge of that trial.

The Charge Against Paul (Acts 18.13-.17)

In the trial before Gallio, Paul's Jewish opponents charge that he is trying to persuade men to worship God in a way that is contrary to the law.

Some scholars have argued that this passage is unhistorical because there was no Roman law that prescribed how God was to be worshipped. However, the language of the charge is ambiguous, probably deliberately. Under Roman law, as we have seen, the prosecutor was always a private party and in this case the prosecution was brought by the local Jewish opponents of Paul. Under the Roman system, the prosecutor always made his charge as broad as possible and it was the responsibility of the magistrate to construe a specific violation of the law. This is the opposite of modern law, in which the prosecutor is required to bring a specific charge.

In short, the Jews were putting forward a broad accusation that they hoped the Proconsul would construe as a specific offense. The question is: which law did they wish to have applied?

During the first century, there were Jewish communities found in all the major cities of the Roman empire. Historical evidence reveals that those communities were protected by an imperial decree which prohibited local political interference with Jewish religious practices. While Paul was not a government official, in the eyes of his Jewish opponents he was meddling with their religion. Indeed, he had split the Jewish community of Corinth into two factions, one Christian and one not. He even taught the spiritual equality of Jew and gentile in Christ, contrary to Jewish religious law.

The Jews may have been asking Gallio to liberalize the meaning of the existing imperial decree so that it applied to private interference with their religion, as well as to governmental interference. Under Roman law, Gallio had the authority to do this. In the end, he did not. Luke records that the trial ended with a ruling by Gallio in Paul's favor.[29]

Following his trial, Paul left Corinth. He took ship at the port of Cenchrea, stopped briefly at Ephesus, then continued by ship to Caesarea. From there, he traveled overland to Antioch, possibly after first visiting Jerusalem (Luke's Greek is unclear). His return to Antioch closes the second missionary journey. Paul has been gone for three years.

Chapter 3

The Third Journey (52-57 AD)

Paul in Ephesus (Acts 18.23-19.12)

Leaving Antioch, Paul sets out on his third missionary journey. He travels again through Galatia and Phrygia, revisiting the churches that he had planted there. Returning to Ephesus, Paul spends two years teaching and preaching in that city. He first operates out of a local synagogue until forced to leave. He then spends part of each day teaching in the lecture hall of Tyrannus. During this period, Paul performs a number of miracles. In one case, sick people are cured simply by having his handkerchiefs and aprons brought to them.

Ephesus was a noted university town, so the fact that Paul ended up teaching in a lecture hall fits the local circumstances. The name Tyrannus is an unusual one, but has been discovered in inscriptions in Ephesus dating to the first century.[1] The detail about Paul's handkerchiefs and aprons is interesting. The handkerchiefs, probably more accurately translated as "head-coverings," along with the aprons, are the work clothes of a leather worker, the trade which Luke has previously identified as Paul's.[2]

The Sons of Sceva (Acts 19.13-.18)

The seven sons of the Jewish High Priest Sceva, who are magicians, begin performing exorcisms in the name of Christ. But they run into trouble when they are set upon and injured by a man whose evil spirit they are trying to exorcise. As he attacks them, he says that he has heard of Jesus, and even of Paul, but who are they?

As noted earlier, the practice of magic was forbidden by Jewish religious law. Nonetheless there were many Jewish magicians in the first century. Such was their influence that pagan magicians often claimed to be Jews. The city of Ephesus was renowned in the ancient world as a center of magic, so again Luke's narrative fits the local circumstances.

However, there are two historical problems with this passage. First, Luke states that Sceva was a Jewish High Priest. History records the name of every Jewish High Priest in the first century, and not one is the Jewish equivalent of the Latin name Sceva. Also, it is extremely improbable that a High Priest of Israel, or his sons, would have ended up as magicians in Ephesus.

On the other hand, both the book of Acts and the Jewish historian Josephus often refer to someone as a High Priest who is simply a member of one of the High Priestly families. Still, it is unlikely that someone from one of those elite families would have become a magician in Ephesus. Quite possibly, Luke means that Sceva was Jewish and that he was the high priest of a local pagan cult. Though this is not the most natural reading of Luke's Greek, it is a possible reading.

A second problem with this passage is that it reads like a popular legend. Sceva has seven sons who are all magicians. They attempt to use the name of Jesus to perform an exorcism and are attacked by the possessed individual, who sets them straight about Christ and Paul. As a result, many of the local magicians become Christians and build a bonfire of their books of magic. They even calculate the monetary value of the works that are burned.

Some scholars discount the historical truth of this event because it reads like a legend. However, there is no real evidence either to confirm or to deny the historical character of this passage.[3]

Erastus (Acts 19.22)

Paul sends two assistants, Erastus and Timothy, to visit the churches in Macedonia.

This is the only time that Erastus is mentioned in Acts, although he is mentioned twice in Paul's letters. At the close of the letter to the Christians at Rome, Paul states that Erastus is the treasurer of the city from which he is writing, which is the city of Corinth. Then, at the end of his second letter to Timothy, Paul records that Erastus stayed behind after Paul left Corinth. In these references to Erastus, and assuming that it is the same individual in each case who is being named, he is mentioned only briefly and in passing. Erastus shows up only briefly in the New Testament.

During an archeological excavation of Corinth in 1929, a first century pavement was uncovered which contains the following inscription: "Erastus, Procurator and Aedile, laid this pavement at his own expense." The pavement was in the public square and Erastus had apparently paid for it in return for his election to the aedileship. The Latin word Aedile denotes an official who, among other duties, is in charge of the financial affairs of the city. Since Paul states that Erastus was the treasurer of Corinth, it would seem that his existence has been confirmed by archeological evidence.

Unfortunately, the matter is more complicated than this. The Greek word that Paul uses to denote "treasurer" (Oikonomos) is not the equivalent of the Latin word Aedile, which refers to a somewhat higher office in ancient municipal government. Of course, Erastus may have been promoted to the office of Aedile after Paul's letter was written. It may also be that Paul, in using the word Oikonomos, is employing a colloquial Greek word as a rough equivalent to the word Aedile. If either one of these explanations is true, the existence of Erastus, his job, and his city of residence, have been confirmed by archeological evidence.

There are further complicating factors. First, the name Erastus was very common in antiquity, so the pavement could have been laid by someone else having that name. Second, there is scholarly disagreement over whether the word Oikonomos could have been used as a colloquial title for Aedile. Third, there is scholarly disagreement over whether someone holding the office of Oikonomos could later have been promoted to Aedile. The weight of historical evidence suggests that the office of Aedile was held only by men of social standing, while those who occupied the socially lower office of Oikonomos were usually not promoted to the rank of Aedile.

In short, the evidence is tantalizingly inconclusive. While it is possible that the Erastus of the Corinthian pavement was the companion of Paul, we cannot know for certain that this is the case.[4]

The Riot at Ephesus (Acts 19.23-.27)

At the end of Paul's two years in Ephesus, an anti-Christian riot takes place. A man named Demetrius, who is a maker of silver shrines, is the instigator. Calling a meeting of shrine makers, he points out that they are losing business because so many people are converting to Christianity.

In the ancient world, Ephesus was known as a center of magic and as a university town. However, the city was most famous because it possessed of one of the seven wonders of the ancient world: the temple of the goddess Artemis, or Diana. One of the major businesses of Ephesus was the making of small shrines, which were sold to visiting pilgrims to place in the temple as offerings. Periodically, the temple priests would clear away the shrines to make room for yet more shrines to be deposited by worshippers.

Archeological excavations have uncovered great numbers of terra-cotta shrines in the vicinity of the temple, but no silver ones. But this is not surprising, since no silver artwork has come down to us from the first century. Anything made with precious metals was sooner or later melted down. An inscription has been discovered in Ephesus that refers to a wealthy Roman who presented a silver image of Diana to the city theater, and there are other local inscriptions that refer to silver statues of Artemis. So it is not improbable that silver shrines were also made.

Interestingly, an inscription has been found in Ephesus, from the first century, that refers to a shrine-maker by the name of Demetrius. Was this the individual named in Acts? Unfortunately, the name Demetrius was extremely common in the ancient world, so the identification cannot be confirmed.

Historical records reveal that guilds of craftsmen played a leading role in the cities of the period, and a disruptive role when their financial interests were at stake. From Ephesian inscriptions, we know that a guild of silversmiths existed in Ephesus at this time.

The complaint about a loss of business because of the large number of conversions to Christianity is echoed in another ancient document. Pliny, the Roman governor of Bithynia at the beginning of the second century, remarks in a letter that the business of supplying fodder for sacrificial animals was rapidly declining in his province, because of the spread of Christianity.[5]

The Theater at Ephesus (Acts 19.28-.34)

The riot spreads through the city. The rioters rush to the theater, dragging two Christians known to be Paul's friends with them. For two hours in the theater, the rioters shout "Great is Artemis of the Ephesians!"

Several ancient inscriptions from Ephesus contain the motto: "Great is Artemis of the Ephesians." Modern excavations reveal that the open-air theater at Ephesus held up to twenty-five thousand people.[6]

The Asiarchs (Acts 19.30-.31)

Paul tries to enter the theater and speak to the crowd, but his friends restrain him. The provincial authorities, who according to Luke were friends of Paul, send him a message begging him not to go into the theater.

In most English translations the title of the provincial authorities is not given. In the Greek, Luke calls them "Asiarchs." Historical evidence shows that the Roman province of Asia was governed by a Proconsul, who had men under him with the title of Asiarchs. It is noteworthy that only in the province of Asia was the office plural. In every other Roman province governed according to this form, a single individual held the post. In Lycia there was a Lyciarch; in Pontus a Pontarch, in Bithynia a Bithynarch. Only in Asia were there Asiarchs.

The duties of the Asiarchs were both political and religious. They administered the imperial cult, which was the worship of the Roman emperor as a god. It may seem strange that the priests in charge of emperor-worship would be Paul's friends, but this was the period before Rome began its persecution of Christians. The first century saw the rapid spread of many religious cults and the tolerance of those cults by the Roman upper class. This stands in sharp contrast to the end of the first century, and afterward, when no priest administering the imperial cult would have associated with Christians. By then, the Roman state was at war with Christianity. Luke's description of Paul's friendship with the Asiarchs can belong only to the middle of the first century.

Recent archeological discoveries have led to a controversy over the office of Asiarch. Some historians argue that the Asiarchs mentioned in Acts may not actually refer to individuals responsible for the imperial cult. Instead, they may have been political officials using a title similar to that used by the priests of the imperial cult. If that is the case, then the Asiarchs mentioned by Luke were, in fact, not pagan priests. However, the evidence is inconclusive.[7]

The People's Clerk (Acts 19.30-.41)

The People's Clerk addresses the mob and tries to calm them.

The title "The People's Clerk" is confirmed by other historical evidence as the official title of the leading magistrate of Ephesus. He was elected annually by the representatives of the people and directed the affairs of the city. One of his duties was presiding over meetings of the citizen assembly.[8]

Twice in this passage, in verses thirty and thirty-two, Luke uses a word to denote the rioters that is the Greek equivalent of a Roman legal term used to describe the citizen assembly of a self-governing city. Scholars have suggested that Luke is being ironic when he calls the rioters a "civic assembly." However, other scholars note that, in verse thirty-nine, the People's Clerk himself uses a Roman legal term to refer to the crowd as an irregular, or unofficial, meeting of the civic assembly. He may have used this word to avoid calling what had happened a riot, in order to put the best face on events.[9]

The speech delivered by the People's Clerk can be paralleled by other speeches made in town meetings during this era. The first century was the final age of local self-government in the Roman empire. By the middle of the second century, city assemblies were nothing more than the rubber stamps of local oligarchies, who ruled in conjunction with the centralized bureaucracy in Rome. Indeed, one can hear the death knell of local democracy in Luke's account of the Clerk's speech. The Clerk's warning that the assembly could be accused of rioting was based on the very real fear that the privileges of Ephesus as a free city might be revoked by the Roman authorities. By calling the rioters an unofficial meeting of the civic assembly, he was trying to put a formal construction on their demonstrations.[10]

Ephesus and the Temple of Artemis (Acts 19.35)

During the Clerk's speech, he states that Ephesus is known as the keeper of the temple of Artemis and of the sacred stone that fell from heaven.

An inscription has been discovered at Ephesus containing the statement that the city is the "Warden of the Temple."[11] As for the sacred stone, there were several temples in antiquity that enshrined meteorites as objects from heaven. Unfortunately, there is no evidence, apart from the testimony of Acts, that Ephesus possessed such a stone. It is possible that the "sacred stone" refers to the stone statue of the goddess that dominated the temple.[12]

The Proconsuls (Acts 19.38)

The People's Clerk tells the multitude that if they want to make an accusation against the Christians they must take their case before the Proconsuls.

It is curious that Luke should use the plural Proconsuls, since under the Roman system there was but one Proconsul to a Senatorial province. The best explanation of this use of the plural form is that the People's Clerk was making a generalizing statement to the effect that "there are Proconsuls for this kind of problem."[13]

The Return to Jerusalem (Acts 20.1-21.8)

Paul leaves Ephesus to make a tour of the churches in Macedonia and Greece, afterward returning to Jerusalem. On the trip to Jerusalem, Paul and his party sail from Philippi after the Jewish feast of unleavened bread, arriving in Troas five days later. From Troas they sail to Assos, then to Mitylene, then anchor off Chios, then off Samos, and then off Miletus. After a delay, they sail to Cos, then to Rhodes, then to Patara. At Patara, they change ships and sail along the southern coast of Cyprus, landing briefly at Tyre while the ship off-loads cargo. From Tyre they sail to Ptolemais and then to Caesarea. They disembark and begin the overland journey to Jerusalem.

The itinerary of this trip, though brief, is quite detailed. This is one of four "we-passages" in Acts, when Luke is writing in the first person. Most of Acts is written in the third person, in which the author says "they did this or that," but here he states that "we" sailed the route, which probably means that he was present on this voyage.

Most of the locations that Luke names are best understood as places that they anchored at the end of each day. This is confirmed by the meteorological evidence. At this time of year (just after the Jewish Passover, in the spring), the wind blows from the North in Mediterranean. It begins early in the morning and dies away in late afternoon. At sunset there is a dead calm, while a gentle breeze blows from the South during the night. This knowledge of the prevailing winds allows us to calculate the time needed to cover the distances between the points that Luke names. They turn out to be distances that would be covered in the course of a day's sailing.

In Acts 20.13, Luke states that Paul temporarily left the ship at Troas. He traveled overland and then met the ship again at Assos. It seems odd that Paul would have been able to travel as fast by land as by ship. However, meteorological data, plus a map of the area, tells us why this happened. Paul's ship had to pass around

Cape Lectum against the prevailing wind, which would have delayed the ship's passage considerably. And the overland distance between Troas and Assos was much shorter than the distance by water. Given these two circumstances, walking to Assos would have been as rapid as sailing there. Though Luke does not tell us why Paul left the ship, it may be that he simply wanted to be on dry land for awhile. In any case, Luke's account fits both the geographical and meteorological data.[14]

The Offices of Bishop and Elder (Acts 20.17-.38)

In Paul's speech to the elders assembled at Miletus, the words elder and bishop are used interchangeably to refer to the same church office. It is only in the first century that they refer to a single office. Beginning early in the second century, the words elder and bishop referred to different offices in the church. This is further evidence that Acts belongs to the first century.[15]

Philip's Daughters (Acts 21.8-.9)

After leaving the ship at Caesarea, Paul and his party stay at the home of Philip the evangelist. According to this passage, Philip had four unmarried daughters who were prophetesses. This is the only reference in the New Testament to Philip's daughters. However, Eusebius, a Christian historian writing in the third century, quotes Papias, a Christian leader of the early second century, as stating that Philip's daughters were still alive in his time. According to Papias, people would journey to visit them, to listen to their stories about the early church.[16]

With Paul's entrance into Jerusalem, the third journey comes to an end.

Chapter 4

Paul's Judean Arrest and Trial (57- 59 AD)

The Nazirite Vow (Acts 21.17-.26)

Following the third missionary journey, Paul visits Jerusalem. However, there are storm clouds on the horizon. Thousands of Jews believe that Jesus is the Messiah, and the church is accepted by other Jews as a sect within Judaism. But this acceptance is based upon Christian Jews' remaining obedient to Jewish religious law.

The Apostles and elders in Jerusalem had long ago decided that non-Jews could become Christians without following Jewish religious practices. However, Paul's Jewish opponents maintain that he has gone beyond this, and teaches that Jews themselves are no longer bound by the religious law. To counter this report, the leaders of the Jerusalem church ask Paul to undertake a vow in the Temple. He joins four other men in a ceremony of ritual purification, while paying their expenses. According to Luke, this ceremony includes the shaving of the participants' heads, and sacrifices at the end of seven days.

Luke is describing the Nazirite vow. The details of this vow can be found in the sixth chapter of the Old Testament book of Numbers (verses thirteen through twenty) and in the thirteenth chapter of Judges (verse seven). The vow is also described in later Jewish rabbinical literature, specifically in the Mishna, Nazir 6.6. There is historical evidence that wealthy Jews in the first century sometimes underwrote the expenses of those who took the vow. Thus Paul's payment of those expenses has a precedent.

The Nazirite vow lasted a month, with the head being shaved at the beginning of the vow. In this passage, Luke seems to say that the vow lasted only seven days. It may be that Paul did not take part in the vow itself, but joined four men who were in the process of completing it. Another possibility is that the men had already completed the vow, but had contracted ritual defilement in the process. Thus Paul would have been participating in a joint purification after the vow.[1]

The Jerusalem Riot (Acts 21.27-.36)

On the seventh day of the purification, some Jews who are visiting from the province of Asia see Paul with the men in the Temple and conclude that he has taken gentiles into the holy place. They cause a riot. The mob enters the Temple and drags Paul outside. Only the swift intervention of Roman troops saves him from death.

Both scripture and independent historical sources record that gentiles were barred from the Inner Court of the Jewish Temple. Inscribed warnings to this effect were posted at the foot of the stairs to the Inner Court, and these inscriptions have been recovered by archaeologists. The Jewish historian Josephus states that the Roman government granted the Jews the right to put even Roman citizens to death for violating this ban. This is the only known instance of a non-Roman authority having capital jurisdiction over a Roman citizen during this era.[2]

The Romans were compelled to make this legal concession because many Jews were fanatical when it came to the Temple. The Romans had a great deal of trouble governing Judea during this era, which was one of continuous Jewish uprisings and revolts against Roman authority. The Romans needed to defuse the potential for violence and the Temple was a flashpoint for Jewish fervor.

Thus it is not surprising that visiting Jews were able to start a riot after seeing Paul in the Temple. Luke's statement that Roman troops swiftly intervened also fits the historical circumstances. During this era, there was a permanent contingent of Roman troops stationed at the fortress of Antonia next door to the Temple. Two flights of steps led down from the fortress to the Outer Court of the Temple. Indeed, Luke tells us that the soldiers "came down" into the riot.[3] The soldiers were led by a tribune and more than one centurion, which means that at least two hundred soldiers were involved.

The Egyptian (Acts 21.37-.38)

Paul is arrested and taken into the fortress. The Tribune asks him if he is the Egyptian who started a revolt by leading four thousand terrorists into the desert.

The Jewish historian Josephus records that an Egyptian claiming to be a prophet appeared in Jerusalem in 54 AD. He led thirty thousand people outside the city walls to the Mount of Olives, while promising that the walls of the city would collapse at his command. Felix, the Roman Procurator of Judea, sent troops against him, with the result that four hundred of the prophet's followers were killed and two hundred were captured. The would-be prophet escaped and was never seen again.

Luke and Josephus are obviously referring to the same event, although their accounts differ in the details. According to Luke, the

Tribune said that four thousand men followed the prophet, while Josephus says that it was thirty thousand. However, in the Greek, the signs for these otherwise very different numbers look almost alike. It is possible that somewhere along the line a copyist's error occurred in either Josephus' or Luke's account. Since it is unlikely that thirty thousand people followed the Egyptian prophet, especially since Josephus gives very low numbers for those who were killed (400) and captured (200), it is probably Josephus' account that is in error.

A second divergence between the two sources is found in Josephus' statement that the Egyptian led his followers to the Mount of Olives, while according to the Tribune, the Egyptian led them into the wilderness. These two statements cannot be reconciled. We can only note that Josephus' histories contain many historical errors, while Luke's writings are consistently reliable in matters of historical detail. If a choice is to be made between the two sources, it is Luke who should be followed.

There is one other minor discrepancy. The Tribune calls the Egyptian's followers terrorists. Terrorists were certainly active in this period, which was only a decade before the general Jewish uprising against Rome. But Josephus clearly distinguishes between terrorist groups and the Egyptian's followers, whom he does not call terrorists. However, a Roman officer would probably call any group opposed to Rome terrorists, so the contradiction between Acts and Josephus is more apparent than real.[4]

Tarsus (Acts 21.39)

In response to the Tribune's question of whether he is the Egyptian terrorist, Paul answers that he is a Jew and a citizen of the city of Tarsus. He then adds that Tarsus is not just any city.

In the first century, it was considered a term of abuse to call someone an Egyptian. Responding to the Tribune, Paul wants to establish his social standing. He states that he is a Jew and a citizen of Tarsus. He does not, at this point, mention that he is a Roman citizen.

Paul's reply fits the circumstances of the middle of the first century. In the first half of the century, few people outside of Italy were Roman citizens. An individual's social status was tied to his citizenship in a particular city or province. Tarsus ranked as a city of some importance in the eastern Roman empire. It was one of a handful of self-governing municipalities and a seat of higher learning.[5]

Gamaliel (Acts 22.3)

With the Tribune's permission, Paul attempts to speak to the mob to calm them. During his speech, Paul states that he was educated in Jerusalem under Gamaliel. Gamaliel is known to history as one of the great Jewish teachers of the first century.[6]

Paul's Roman Citizenship (Acts 22.24-.29)

The Tribune orders Paul to be scourged to discover why the Jews were rioting against him. In response, Paul reveals his Roman citizenship. The Tribune is surprised at this, and remarks that he had to pay a great deal of money to obtain his citizenship. Paul replies that he was born a Roman.

According to the historian Dio Cassius, the selling of Roman citizenship was widespread, and a political scandal, during the reign of the Emperor Claudius. He states that it was suppressed only after Nero became emperor. Other historical sources record that the sale of Roman citizenship continued under every emperor during this era.

Luke tells us (Acts 23.26) that the Tribune's name was Claudius Lysias. Since it was the practice of new Roman citizens to take the name of the ruling emperor, the Tribune's name is further evidence that he had become a Roman citizen during this era. Some historians have argued that the Tribune would not have publicly admitted that he had bought his citizenship. However, Lysias was not making a public statement; he was engaged in a private conversation with Paul.

Scholars have also questioned whether Lysias would have revealed this information, even privately, to someone that he did not know. But clearly Lysias is trying to draw Paul out about the source of his own citizenship. In first century Roman courts, legal judgments were inevitably biased by the social standing of the person being charged. If Paul had bought his citizenship, he and the Tribune were social equals. But if Paul had been born a Roman, Lysias was his social inferior. The Tribune would have had to tread very carefully in dealing with Paul, especially since he had placed Paul in chains and threatened him with torture. It was illegal to do either of these things to a Roman citizen.

This brief passage demonstrates the historical accuracy of the narrative. If someone had invented this exchange between Lysias and Paul at a later date, he would never have included the conversation that is recorded here. By the end of the first century, Roman citizenship was so widespread that the situation described in this passage no longer existed. By that time, a majority of the empire's population had become citizens and citizenship had lost its earlier prerogatives. The problem of acquiring citizenship, as well as its illegal sale, belongs to the middle of the first century, and to no other period.[7]

Ananias the High Priest (Acts 22.30-23.5)

In order to frame an accusation against Paul, the Tribune commands the Jewish Sanhedrin to meet, then brings Paul before them. Paul is allowed to speak and begins by saying that his conscience is clear before God. This prompts the High Priest Ananias to order those sitting next to Paul to strike him. Paul responds by stating that God will strike Ananias for presuming to

*judge according to the Law while violating that Law. Paul is
informed that it is the High Priest to whom he is speaking, and he
apologizes. Paul then states that he did not know that it was the
High Priest.*

The Jewish historian Josephus provides us with some of the
details of the career of Ananias. He was appointed High Priest in
47 AD and imprisoned at Rome in 52 AD on a charge of being
responsible for uprisings in Judea. He was eventually acquitted
and restored by the Romans to authority in Jerusalem. He was later
assassinated by Jewish terrorists in 66 AD for siding with the
Romans during the Jewish revolt. Josephus states that Ananias was
known for his quick temper, which is also revealed in this passage
in Acts.[8]

Some scholars have argued that this passage cannot be
authentic, since Paul would have recognized the distinctive dress
of the High Priest. At a formal meeting of the Sanhedrin, the High
Priest would indeed be recognizable by his dress, as well as by the
fact that he was presiding. But this was not a formal meeting of the
Sanhedrin. Luke states that the Tribune summoned the Sanhedrin
to discover the charges against Paul. Since the Tribune was a
pagan, his presence at the meeting means that the Sanhedrin could
not have been in formal session.

There is also another reason why this could not have been a
formal meeting. Paul was a Roman citizen, which means that he
could only be tried by the Roman governor of Palestine. The
Sanhedrin had no legal authority over him.

In short, there is no reason to believe that the High Priest would
have been distinguishable from the rest of the assembly. He may
even have kept in the background, quite deliberately, while letting
others speak.[9]

Some scholars have argued that this passage in Acts is
untrustworthy because it parallels Jesus' appearance before the
High Priest on the night before His crucifixion. In that case, as
well, the High Priest ordered Jesus struck for His words and Jesus
replied in much the same way as Paul did. Then, after being told

that He was speaking to the High Priest, Jesus apologized, stating that He did not know that it was the High Priest.

The two accounts are obviously similar. But there are also decisive differences. The reason Jesus did not recognize the High Priest is because He was the subject of a midnight interrogation that did not involve the Sanhedrin at all. The interrogation was illegal and conducted by only a handful of people, none of whom introduced themselves. Luke undoubtedly recognized the parallels between these two incidents, and probably recorded it for that very reason. But other than the coincidence that both Jesus and Paul were struck at the order of a High Priest, and their similar responses, the incidents are completely different. Paul, unlike Jesus, was appearing in broad daylight as part of a public inquiry. Nor was he crucified as the result of that inquiry. Instead, Paul remained a prisoner for two years in Judea and was afterward sent to Rome for trial before the emperor.

Pharisees and Sadducees (Acts 23.6-.10)

During his appearance before the Sanhedrin, Paul manages to divide his enemies by stating that he is on trial because he is a Pharisee who believes in the resurrection of the dead. The Pharisees immediately take Paul's side against the Sadducees, who do not believe in the resurrection of the dead.

The theological dispute over the resurrection of the dead was one of the central issues dividing the Pharisees and Sadducees. Scholars have argued that this picture of Paul's dividing his Jewish enemies so easily is too unbelievable to be true. They argue that even though the Pharisees and Sadducees were opposed on the doctrine of the resurrection, they were even more opposed to Christianity – and especially to Paul.

However, this argument attempts to prove too much. To begin with, it assumes that the two main Jewish parties during this period detested Christianity more than they detested each other. The historical record suggests that the church in Jerusalem had reached an understanding with Judaism during this period, and that the church was regarded as a Jewish sect. This is implied by the book of Acts on several occasions, and is also implied by the Jewish historian Josephus.

Josephus records the martyrdom of James, the brother of Jesus and the leader of the Jerusalem church. This event occurred only a few years after Paul's appearance before the Sanhedrin. Josephus writes that James' execution by the Sadducean High Priest, during a temporary lapse of Roman authority, provoked outrage among the Jews in Jerusalem. He states that James was respected by the Jews for his strict adherence to Jewish religious law, and for his holy life. Following the re-establishment of Roman authority in Jerusalem, the Jewish leadership called on the Romans to punish the High Priest for the execution of James.

Clearly, it is impossible for us today to know the nature of the political and religious tensions within the Sanhedrin at this time. But anyone who follows modern politics knows that the strangest alliances are possible in the right circumstances. Paul's stratagem to divide the Jewish assembly is so transparent that it must have been a pretext. The Pharisees, while not wanting to defend Paul directly, may have regarded the Sadducean prosecution as a power play that was aimed at both the Christians and themselves. Their need for a pretext to intervene on Paul's behalf may even have been communicated to Paul by a Jewish Christian with ties to the Pharisees. What better issue could be thought of than the doctrine that both the Pharisees and Christians held in common, yet was rejected by the Sadducees, a belief in the resurrection of the dead?

Of course, this is conjecture. Yet it is a plausible conjecture, since experience suggests that political events are often the result of such calculations.[10]

The Assassination Attempt (Acts 23.12-.30)

Following Paul's appearance before the Sanhedrin, a plot is hatched to assassinate him. The Tribune is informed and decides to send Paul immediately to Caesarea, to be tried by the Roman governor. An escort of about five hundred men is detailed to accompany him on the first leg of the journey, to the city of Antipatris. The Tribune writes a letter to the governor about Paul, which is reproduced by Luke.

A five-hundred-man escort to protect a single individual would seem be excessive, especially since this was half the Roman garrison of Jerusalem. Some scholars have argued that it is improbable that such a large force would have been sent to accompany Paul. On the other hand, Judea was on the verge of revolt throughout this period. Local uprisings, led by Jewish terrorists, occurred repeatedly. Paul's large escort, which accompanied him only on the first stage of the journey, would surely have discouraged any attempt to cause trouble. The other details contained in this passage – the exact time of the escort's departure from Jerusalem, the number of mounted soldiers, and the numbers and kinds of other troops – all point to a real event.

Some historians have objected that the infantry, since it was on foot, could not have covered the distance to Antipatris (approximately 35 miles) in a single night. It is true that twenty miles a day was the usual standard of Roman march, but a forced march of 35 miles, even at night, was not impossible. There are examples from Roman history of such marches. On the other hand, it may be that Luke simply does not mention that the infantry turned back to Jerusalem once Paul was safely outside the city. The rest, who were mounted, could have easily reached Antipatris in a single night.[11]

The contents of the Tribune's letter, as recorded by Luke, reflect the Roman legal process. The letter begins with an account of the preliminary interrogation of the prisoner and ends with the statement of the Tribune that he has instructed Paul's accusers to make their charges before the governor. Nine separate Roman legal terms have been found in this letter, and modern experts in ancient Roman law argue that this passage is probably a copy of at least part of the actual letter.

In the letter, the Tribune states that when he learned that a Roman citizen was about to be killed by a Jewish mob he took some soldiers and rescued him. This contradicts Luke's account, which says that the Tribune did not know who Paul was when he intervened to arrest him. Of course, by saying that he knew that he was rescuing a Roman citizen, the Tribune puts himself in a favorable light.[12]

Roman Law: A Note

With Paul's arrival in Caesarea, the trial before the Roman Procurator begins. But before turning to Luke's account of that trial, we need to understand something of the nature of Roman law during this period.

Before the first century, if a Roman citizen was charged with a crime, he had to be tried in the city of Rome no matter where the charge was made. The expansion of the empire eventually made this impractical. By the first century, Roman provincial governors were given the authority to try Roman citizens who committed crimes within their jurisdictions. However, such was the conservative nature of Roman law that any citizen tried by a Roman governor still had the right to appeal his case directly to the emperor's court in Rome. He could make this appeal either during his provincial trial or after a verdict had been reached.

By the close of the first century, so many people had become Roman citizens that the right of appeal to Rome disappeared in practice, even though it remained on the books. Paul's appeal, which he exercised after two years of inconclusive trial in Judea, fits the legal system of the middle of the first century.

Another important point is that mid-first century Roman governors were required to enforce a two-tier system of law. First, there was the *Ordo Iudicorium Publicorum* ("The List of National Courts"). This was a compilation of serious crimes against the Roman state. Second, there were ordinary crimes as defined in a particular province. A Roman citizen under indictment could be tried according to whichever of the two categories a Roman governor found more relevant.

The governor had complete discretion in his interpretation of these laws. In theory, he possessed the same authority within his province that the emperor possessed over the empire. That is to say, he had absolute power. However, the governor was also subject to the oversight of the emperor and the Senate, so this theoretically unlimited power had real limitations. In judging any case, he had to take account of the political effects of his decision. And in the middle of the first century, he did not possess absolute authority, even in theory, over a Roman citizen, whose rights had to be respected.[13]

Paul's Home Province (Acts 23.33-.35)

Paul is brought before the Roman Procurator Felix. Felix reads the Tribune's letter and asks Paul what province he is from. Paul replies that he is from Cilicia. Felix states that he will hear the case when Paul's accusers arrive, and dismisses him.

From Roman historians we know that Felix was Procurator of Judea at this time. However, Luke's account of this initial interview is somewhat mysterious. Why does Felix ask Paul what province he is from? And why, after Paul tells him, does Felix dismiss him until his accusers arrive? Luke provides no answer to this question. It is only when we consult first century Roman law that we discover the answer.

The legal principle behind the Procurator's question was called the *forum domecilii*. Applicable only to *Ordo* offenses (crimes against the Roman state), this principle permitted the governor of the province in which a Roman citizen was arrested to transfer the case to the province that the citizen was from. The decision to make this transfer was entirely in the hands of the arresting governor, and gave him the opportunity to dispose of cases that he did not wish to try. This legal principle first appeared in Roman law during the first quarter of the first century and then disappeared by the end of the century, when citizenship became so common that it no longer applied.

Since the Romans always had problems dealing with the Jews, why didn't Felix take this opportunity to transfer Paul's trial to Cilicia? The answer is that Cilicia was probably not a Roman province at this time. Only a few years before Paul's trial, Cilicia's status was that of a dependency of the Roman Legate of Syria. A few years after Paul's trial, Cilicia was a Roman province. The problem is that we do not know the date at which Cilicia became a province. This passage in Acts implies that Cilicia was not yet a province at the time of Paul's trial.

Felix could have transferred Paul's case to the Roman Legate of Syria, who was responsible for Cilicia. However, the Legate was also responsible for Judea. This means Felix would have been transferring the case to his superior. This is probably not something that he would want to do. So he placed Paul under house arrest until the beginning of the trial.[14]

Tertullus' Speech and Paul's Reply (Acts 24.1-.21)

The High Priest Ananias arrives in Caesarea. He is accompanied by some of the Jewish elders and by a lawyer named Tertullus. The trial begins and Tertullus rises to make the Jewish case against Paul. Afterward, Paul replies.

In his speech to the Procurator, Tertullus accuses Paul of no specific violations of the law, but makes general accusations about his conduct. As previously noted, this kind of legal argument conforms to Roman judicial procedure. The task of the prosecuting party is to make the charges as broad as possible, while the responsibility of the Procurator is to construe a specific violation of the law.

According to modern specialists in Roman law, Tertullus is accusing Paul of an offense against the Ordo – that is to say, a crime against the Roman state. Some scholars argue that an Ordo offense required the prosecutor to make a specific accusation. It is true that specific charges were required for Ordo cases brought before judges within the city walls of Rome, but there is no evidence that this was a feature of Roman law in the provinces. Apart from this passage in Acts, there is no historical account of a provincial governor conducting a trial for an Ordo offense during this era.

Indeed, from historical accounts of provincial trials on other matters, there is reason to believe that an Ordo trial would have been conducted differently by a Roman governor from the way it would have been conducted by the courts at Rome. Since the governor embodied the Imperium, and had an authority that was theoretically absolute, he would not necessarily have been bound by the technical requirements that applied to judges in Rome. However, in the final analysis, there is simply not enough evidence to decide this matter. This passage in Acts represents the only first century account of an Ordo offense tried in a provincial court.

An important feature of Tertullus' speech against Paul is found in the fifth verse. He accuses Paul of "stirring up a plague and disturbances for Jews throughout the world." These words echo a phrase found in a letter written by the Emperor Claudius to the citizens of Alexandria, Egypt, only a few years before Paul's trial. In that letter, Claudius condemns the political activities of the Jewish community in that city, charging them with "stirring up a universal plague throughout the world."

Actually, it was common for first century Romans to accuse Jews of fomenting civil disorder in the empire, a charge that was not always unjustified. It should be remembered that Paul is not so much a Christian in the eyes of the Roman authorities as he is just another Jew. Of course, it is fascinating to consider that a lawyer representing the Jewish elite of Judea would employ an anti-Jewish argument against Paul. However, the Sadducean party, which controlled the Sanhedrin, was pro-Roman and hated by other Jews.

Paul replies to Tertullus and points out that it was Jews from the province of Asia who made the original accusation against him. He states that it is those individuals who should be brought forward to prosecute him.

Paul's argument goes to the core of the legal problem, and he is making a serious charge of his own. Under Roman law, any accuser who brought a charge, and then abandoned it, was liable for criminal penalties himself. This is why he asks where the Asian Jews are, since they are the ones who made the original accusations against him.

Because those Jews have disappeared, Tertullus' strategy is to frame the accusation against Paul on some other foundation. He brings political charges against Paul, while using theological evidence. Paul's strategy is just the opposite. He seeks to portray Tertullus' charges as entirely theological, and thus as irrelevant to the court.[15]

Felix and Drusilla (Acts 24.22-.26)

Following the arguments, Felix concludes the hearing. He states that he will decide the case after the Tribune arrives to testify. Still under house arrest, Paul is visited by Felix and his Jewish wife, Drusilla, who come to talk with him about Christ. According to Luke, Felix was also looking for a bribe to decide the case in Paul's favor.

There are several things in this passage that are confirmed by historical evidence. First, the delay of the trial until the arrival of the Tribune fits the procedures of Roman law. Lysias Claudius would be considered the only independent witness to the facts of the case.[16] Second, both the Jewish historian Josephus and the Roman historian Suetonius state that Drusilla was Felix's third wife. She was married to him at the time of Paul's trial.[17] Third, Josephus and the Roman historian Tacitus record that Felix took bribes.[18]

Felix Replaced as Procurator (Acts 24.27)

Paul remains a prisoner for two years, while Felix continually delays the conclusion of the trial. According to Luke, he refuses to decide the case in order to gain favor with the Jews. However, conditions change when he is replaced as Procurator by Porcius Festus.

Felix was indeed replaced by Porcius Festus. According to Josephus, Felix was recalled to Rome under indictment because of his brutal intervention in a riot between Jews and gentiles in the city of Caesarea. He was prosecuted for his actions by some of the Jews involved. Josephus also states that those Jews were not supported in their prosecution by the Sadducean hierarchy in Jerusalem, who supported Felix instead. Thus Luke's statement that Felix left Paul a prisoner in order to gain favor with the Jewish leadership appears in a new light.[19]

It was not particularly unusual that Paul was kept a prisoner for two years while awaiting Felix's decision. So long as Paul did not exercise his right of appeal, he could be held indefinitely. Under Roman law, there was no time limit in conducting a trial. Since Paul's imprisonment in Caesarea consisted of house arrest, and he could work and meet with people as he chose, he decided to stay the course. [20]

Paul did not want to take his case to Rome if that could be avoided. For that would directly involve the imperial courts, and possibly the emperor, in a case that Paul considered to be a purely religious matter. Appealing to Rome meant increasing the probability of having the case being treated as a political matter.

This passage does present one historical difficulty. According to Josephus, Felix was brought to Rome for trial, but escaped punishment because of the political influence of his brother Pallas. According to the Roman historian Tacitus, Pallas was removed from power by the Emperor Nero in 55 AD, which would be the year before Paul's Judean trial. Some scholars argue that this means that Felix must have returned to Rome before his brother's removal from office, which proves that Luke's chronology of events is wrong.

Other scholars argue that though Pallas was removed from office before Paul's trial, this does not mean that his political influence came to an end. Pallas was executed by Nero in 62 AD, or several years after Paul's Judean trial. This suggests that Pallas still possessed enough political influence for Nero to want to get rid of him. Although out of office by the time of Felix's recall, Pallas could still have provided political assistance to his brother. Thus the claim that a contradiction exists between Luke and Tacitus is not proven.[21]

Paul's Appeal to the Emperor   (Acts 25.1-.12)

The new Procurator, Porcius Festus, wants to move Paul's trial back to Jerusalem. Paul objects and immediately exercises his right of appeal to the emperor. Festus consults with his advisors, then states that Paul will be sent to Rome.

Because Festus consults with his advisors before saying that Paul will be sent to Rome, some scholars have argued that Luke is claiming that Festus had the power to grant, or deny, Paul's appeal. However, first century Roman law is clear. A citizen's right to appeal to the emperor was absolute. Festus had no choice in the matter. Thus, these scholars charge, Luke is wrong for suggesting that Festus had that power.

The problem with this argument is that Luke does not actually state that Festus granted Paul's appeal. Luke only says that Festus first consulted with his advisors, then announced that he was sending Paul to Rome. Under Roman law, a provincial governor could either send a prisoner to Rome immediately after his appeal, or he could continue to investigate the case. It was probably the question of whether to continue the investigation that was the reason for Festus' consultation with his advisors.[22]

Agrippa and Bernice (Acts 25.13)

King Herod Agrippa and Bernice, his consort, arrive in Caesarea to visit the newly appointed Roman Procurator.

This would be King Herod Agrippa II. Bernice was his sister. At the time of Paul's trial, she was living with Agrippa and the nature of their relationship was one of the public scandals of that era. The Roman comic writer Juvenal refers to it in one of his satires.

Just a few years before Paul's trial, Bernice was married and living with her husband. A few years after Paul's trial, she was married once more and no longer living with her brother. The short period of time that she was living with her brother corresponds to the period in which Paul was a prisoner in Caesarea.[23]

People and Events: A Note

Throughout the narrative of Paul's Judean arrest and trial, Luke refers to a number of people and events whose existence and relationships are confirmed by the secular histories of the time.

First, there is the Egyptian prophet and his revolt, which occurred only a few years before these events. Second, there is the Jewish High Priest Ananias, who was indeed the High Priest at the time of Paul's arrest and trial. Third, there is the Roman Procurator Felix, who was governor of Judea and married to Drusilla at the time of Paul's trial, this being his third marriage and Drusilla's second. Fourth, Bernice had, by this time, been married twice and was living with her brother, King Herod Agrippa. A few years after Paul's trial she was married again. Fifth, the Procuratorship of Porcius Festus overlaps the chronology of Paul's trial.

Sixth, there is Luke's description of the social position of the Tribune Lysias Claudius, who bought his citizenship, which is an event that belongs to the middle of the first century. Seventh, there are the legal details of Paul's trial, which fit the middle of the first

century and no other period. Eighth, Paul's home territory of
Cilicia was probably not yet a province, which is why Felix did not
transfer the trial there. Ninth, Luke's references to certain personal
characteristics – that Felix was bribable and that Ananias was
easily angered – are confirmed by other historical sources.

All these things taken together demonstrate Luke's accuracy as
an historian.[24]

Audience with Festus and Agrippa (Acts 26.1-.32)

*Paul is brought before Festus and King Agrippa to speak about
Christ. During his discourse, Paul tells about his early life and his
persecution of the Christians. He states that, under the authority
of the High Priest, he put Christians in jail and even voted to put
some of them to death.*

This statement presents an historical problem, since Rome
(with only one known exception) did not permit non-Roman
authorities to exercise the death penalty. Capital punishment was a
power reserved to Roman authority alone. As the gospels correctly
note, Jesus had to be crucified by Pontius Pilate because the Jews
could not legally kill Him. Thus Luke would seem to be in error in
quoting Paul as stating that he voted to put Christians to death.

However, historians have pointed out that civil lynchings were
common during this era, and were winked at by local Roman
authorities. When Paul states that he voted to put Christians to
death, he may be referring to his participation in an extra-legal
conspiracy, sanctioned by the Jewish leadership and ignored by the
Romans.[25]

Another possible contradiction exists in verse thirty-two.
Following Paul's speech, Agrippa turns to Festus and says: "This
man could have been released if he had not appealed to the
emperor." Some scholars argue that this statement is unhistorical,
since Paul could still have been released by Festus even after
making his appeal. But Agrippa is probably referring to the

political realities of the situation. If Festus had released Paul after his appeal, he would have been deciding that the emperor's court should not be allowed to hear Paul's case. He would also have raised the question of why he had not released Paul prior to that appeal. Judicially, he could have released Paul. Politically, it was probably impossible for him to do so.

With this, we reach the conclusion of Paul's Judean trial. The twenty-seventh chapter of Acts opens with Paul, under guard, being placed on a ship bound for Rome.

Chapter 5

Paul's Voyage to Rome and Shipwreck (59-60 AD)

The Augustan Cohort (Acts 27.1-.2)

Paul, along with some other prisoners, is handed over to a Centurion of the Augustan Cohort. Boarding ship at Caesarea, Paul is accompanied by two companions, Aristarchus and the author of Acts.

Ancient inscriptions attest to the existence of an auxiliary legion called the "Augustan Cohort" in Palestine during the first century. However, historical evidence suggests that the duty of escorting prisoners was reserved to *legionary* centurions alone. Thus a centurion from an auxiliary legion could not have been Paul's escort. It is possible that Luke's reference is not to the auxiliary legion located in Palestine. The phrase "Augustan Cohort" simply means "the troop of the emperor." He may be referring to a group of centurions on detached service, one of whose responsibilities was to escort prisoners. Such units existed during the second century, although there is no evidence for them in the first century. In short, there is not enough evidence either to confirm or to deny Luke's reference to the "Augustan Cohort."[1]

Luke states that he and Aristarchus accompanied Paul on the voyage. How likely is it that a prisoner, even if he were a Roman citizen, would have been permitted to take friends with him to Rome? The only other evidence on this question is found in a letter written by Pliny, who was the Roman governor of Bithynia fifty years after Paul's voyage. He tells of a prisoner sent to Rome who was permitted to take his slaves with him. It should be noted that Paul's ship was a public conveyance and that other passengers were aboard. So it is possible that Luke and Aristarchus were passengers as well.[2]

Caesarea to Myra (Acts 27.3-.5)

Leaving Caesarea, the ship arrives in Sidon the next day. After leaving Sidon, the prevailing winds force them to pass east and north of Cyprus on their way west to Myra.

The distance between Caesarea and Sidon is 67 land miles, and to travel that distance in a single day requires a leading wind. The prevailing wind at that time of year (Acts 27.9 reveals that it was early fall) was from the west. This would have allowed them to cover the distance in the time stated.

Luke records that the prevailing wind forced the ship to pass east and north of the island of Cyprus. Both meteorological and nautical evidence confirm this statement. Given the prevailing west wind, they would have had to pass north of the island to continue west.

It was only after their vessel reached the Cilician coast that they could make headway against the wind. At that point, they would be aided by currents running along the coast, as well as by land breezes emanating from the Turkish land mass. Other ancient sources confirm that ships were forced to this route when the wind was from the west. The Greek writer Lucian records that it took his ship nine days to sail from Sidon to Myra by this route.[3]

The Egyptian Grain Ship (Acts 27.6)

Landing at Myra, the Centurion transfers Paul and the other prisoners to an Alexandrian grain ship bound for Rome.

Myra was a major port in the eastern empire. It lay directly north of Alexandria, Egypt, on the far side of the Mediterranean. An Egyptian ship sailing for Rome would have to sail north to Myra at this time of year, because it was impossible to sail directly northwest to Rome. The prevailing wind from the west forced ships sailing from Egypt to Rome to follow this indirect route.

This presents us with a series of interesting evidential coincidences. The same westerly wind that accounted for the shortness of Paul's trip to Sidon is the wind that required his ship to sail north of Cyprus, and is also the wind that brought the Egyptian ship to Myra. All three of these events confirm the direction of the prevailing wind.

Luke, in Acts 27.1, states that the ship they boarded in Caesarea was sailing for ports along the coast of the province of Asia. In other words, the ship was not bound for Rome, but was making ports of call along the southern coast of what today is Turkey. The harbor at Myra was one of the great trans-shipping ports of the ancient Mediterranean. Thus it makes sense that Paul and the others would leave the coastal vessel there and board the larger grain ship for the final leg of the voyage to Rome.[4]

From Myra to Crete (Acts 27.7-.8)

The Egyptian grain ship leaves Myra, then sails slowly westward for several days. Finally, they stand off the town of Cnidus, having reached that point only with the greatest difficulty. Because the wind is against them, the ship's captain decides to sail southwest, in order to pass to the south of the island of Crete. After passing Cape Salome on the eastern end of the island, they make their way along the southern coast. It is with difficulty that they reach the harbor called Fair Havens.

The distance from Myra to Cnidus is 130 land miles. The ship could have covered that distance in a single day with a favoring wind. Luke says that it took several days, which again confirms that the prevailing wind was against them. In sailing west to Cnidus, they were leaving the shelter of the Turkish land mass.

Finding it impossible to proceed any farther west at Cnidus, the ship turned to the southwest to get behind Crete. This change in course is an important piece of evidence. It tells us that the wind had shifted, though Luke does not actually say that this occurred. The wind must now have been blowing from the northwest, since if it had been blowing from the west they could have crossed the Aegean Sea north of Crete. More importantly, a westerly wind would have made it impossible for them to sail to the southwest to get behind Crete.

Luke does not mention this change of wind direction, but he records its consequences. Meteorological evidence reveals that in late summer and early fall the prevailing wind often shifts to the northwest in the Mediterranean. Since this was the time of year they sailed, this is a further confirmation that the wind was now blowing from the northwest.

There is another interesting piece of nautical evidence. Had Paul's ship turned to the southwest at any point between Myra and Cnidus, they would never have reached Crete. The islands in their path would have prevented them from turning to get behind Crete until the angle of descent was such that the northwest wind would have made that maneuver impossible. Southern Crete could not be reached by an ancient sailing ship from any point along their route, except by turning southwest at Cnidus.

After Paul's ship reached Cape Salome on the eastern edge of Crete, they ran along the southern coast and used the island as a shelter from the wind. Luke records that it was with difficulty that they reached the harbor of Fair Havens. He then states that they halted there, but does not say why.

Meteorological and nautical evidence tells us why. Looking at the map of southern Crete (on page 157), you will notice that Cape Matala lies just four miles west of Fair Havens harbor. At the Cape, the coast curves to the north. Had their ship sailed past Cape Matala, they would have been exposed to the northwest wind and would have found it impossible to continue westward. The reason for their halt at Fair Havens was to wait for a change in the wind. Luke's statement that they made the harbor at Fair Havens with difficulty also fits the evidence. A sailing ship working its way westward against a northwest wind, even under the shelter of Crete, would have had problems reaching Fair Havens.[5]

Sailing to Phoenix (Acts 27.9-.12)

It was past the Jewish Day of Atonement, or mid-October, when the wind finally changed. A fair wind from the south began to blow and the captain decided to make for a better harbor at Phoenix, on the western end of Crete. Because of the lateness of the season, his decision was controversial.

During the winter, no ships sailed on the Mediterranean. As Luke records, they could either winter at Fair Havens or use the temporary southern wind to make for Phoenix. Luke maintains that Fair Havens was not a good winter harbor, and that the captain and the sailors wanted to try for Phoenix. The argument against sailing for Phoenix was the lateness of the season, with the real possibility of a sudden, adverse wind that could wreck the ship.[6]

There are two pieces of evidence that bear on this passage. First, although Fair Havens is not the best of harbors, modern surveys reveal that it is a safe winter harbor. Second, Luke implies that the Centurion made the final decision to sail. Although it may seem odd to us today that an army commander would make this decision, in the Roman military there was no separation between land and sea forces. The Roman navy was an extension of the army, with army commanders serving as naval officers.

However, this was a private ship and not a naval vessel. Some scholars argue that the captain, who was the owner of the ship, would have made the decision, rather than the Centurion. But inscriptional evidence from the first century indicates that ship owners who took part in the vital grain trade between Egypt and Rome were generally licensed as agents of the Roman state. They were a kind of public utility and were under strict government regulation. Since the Centurion represented the Roman state, his permission may have been needed to sail.[7]

Scholars have also argued that the ship's owner would not have wanted to risk his ship so late in the season. However, according to the Roman historian Suetonius, throughout this era the city of Rome faced continuing shortages of food during the winter months. Thus the Emperor Claudius offered substantial bonuses to ship owners who took the chance of sailing late in the season. This may have been the reason for the captain's willingness to try for the harbor at Phoenix. From there, it would have been possible to make for Rome if the weather held.[8]

The location of Phoenix's harbor remains something of a mystery. There are two bays at the western end of southern Crete, only one of which corresponds to Luke's description as being open to the southwest and northwest. Today this bay is not deep enough to serve as a harbor, though it may have been of sufficient depth two thousand years ago. A geological survey has established that parts of the western coast of Crete are twenty feet higher today than in antiquity, the result of earthquake activity over the centuries. The line of the bay has been traced and has been shown to have been deeper in Paul's time. Whether it was deep enough for use as a harbor remains an open question.

The second bay, which has a deep harbor and is used by ships today, faces the opposite direction from that recorded by Luke. If this is the bay for which Paul's ship was heading, then Luke's description of it is wrong. But then, Paul's ship never reached Phoenix, so Luke may have erred because he never saw the harbor. On the other hand, he may not have been mistaken. There is simply not enough evidence to decide which of the two bays was the site of the ancient harbor.[9]

The Gale (Acts 27.13-.20)

In verse thirteen, Luke says that after leaving Fair Havens the ship sailed close to shore. While this passage demonstrates Luke's reliability as an observer, it shows that he was no sailor. The ship did not sail close to shore on purpose. They had no choice in the matter. Cape Matala lies four miles south by west of Fair Havens, with the wind now coming from the south. Because ancient ships could not lie closer to the wind than seven points, they would have had a struggle to keep the ship from being blown against the coast until finally rounding the Cape.[10]

From Cape Matala, it was 34 miles to Phoenix, with the southern wind now favoring their course. They should have reached the harbor in a few hours. Instead, there was a violent change in the weather. A gale suddenly roared down on them from Crete's seven-thousand-foot tall mountains, forcing them to turn and run before the wind.

Luke records that the sailors called this wind Euraquilo. An unusual name, it has been found in one ancient inscription and is a slang compound of Greek and Latin. The Greek Erus (east) and the Latin Aquilo (north) translates as "northeaster," a strong winter wind. Meteorological evidence reveals that a sudden change from a mild southerly wind to a violent northeasterly wind often occurs in late fall in the eastern Mediterranean.[11]

According to Luke, they ran before the wind to avoid capsizing, then found temporary shelter behind the small island of Clauda, southwest of Cape Matala. Luke says nothing about an attempt to anchor there, which indeed would have been impossible, since the only anchorage on that island is open to the east-northeast.

Temporarily safe behind Clauda, they had two choices. First, they could turn and run before the storm once more. In that case, they would be faced with the eventual possibility of the ship's wrecking on the north African coast. Luke mentions the fear of the sailors that they would be driven onto that coast. Their second choice – which is the course that they took – was to secure the ship, point it into the wind, and drift slowly westward in the teeth of the storm.

Luke does not actually state that they pointed the ship into the wind. He says only that they decided to drift with the storm. But for a sailing vessel to drift in a gale without capsizing, it must either face toward the wind or away from it. We know that they did not face the ship away from the wind, because in that case they would have drifted slowly to southwest, to the African coast. Since Luke records that they wrecked on the island of Malta, to the northwest, we know that they faced the ship into the wind.

While they were temporarily behind Clauda, three distinct operations were performed. First, with difficulty, they hauled in the small boat that, like other ancient ships, they towed on a line behind them. Second, they took ropes and undergirded the ship to strengthen it against the waves. Third, and most importantly, they trimmed the sail. This was probably done first, although Luke mentions it last. Each of these actions are steps that would have been taken to secure an ancient ship in a storm.

In modern translations of this passage, the lowering of the mainsail is usually not mentioned. Instead, Luke is quoted as saying that they lowered a sea anchor. However, the literal translation of Luke's Greek is that they lowered "the ship's gear," which would include the mainsail.[12]

The Adria (Acts 27.27)

Luke states that the ship drifted on the Adria for fourteen days, the gale continuing the whole time. Today, the Adriatic Sea is a body of water between Italy and the Balkans, a finger-like extension of the Mediterranean Sea. But in antiquity, the term denoted a more extensive area. In the second century AD, the geographer Pausanias and the astronomer Ptolemy both refer to the

Mediterranean as far south as Sicily and Crete as being the "Adria."[13]

Drifting 14 Days in the Storm

Luke records that the ship drifted for fourteen days in the gale and then shipwrecked on the island of Malta, halfway across the Mediterranean. This account of a fourteen day gale, followed by a shipwreck on a remote island, reads like a tall tale. However, the meteorological and nautical evidence demonstrates, in rather spectacular fashion, that these events must have occurred just as Luke records them.

The most important piece of evidence is the compass bearing of the gale. This bearing can be established by means of three separate calculations.

First, Luke states that Euraquilo struck shortly after they left Fair Havens. In other words, the ship must have been less than halfway to their intended destination at Phoenix. This would put it somewhere between Cape Matala and a point seventeen miles W.N.W. of the Cape when the gale struck.

Second, there is the relation of the island of Clauda to this start point. Cape Matala is on a bearing of east 7 degrees north from the eastern edge of Clauda, while the halfway point to Phoenix is east 40 degrees north. For the ship to get behind Clauda, Euraquilo must have been blowing from a point somewhere between these two bearings. The point midway between these two figures is east 25 degrees north (or E.N.E. 1/4 N.). This cannot be more than a point and a half off the actual direction of the wind.

Third, Luke states that when they got behind Clauda, the sailors were afraid that they would be blown onto the Syrtis sandbanks of the north Africa coast. However, for them to have been blown onto those banks from Clauda, Euraquilo would have had to have been blowing from a point somewhere between east 18 degrees north and east 37 degrees north. The point midway between these figures is east 27 degrees north. This figure is only 1/4 point off the mean figure of the previous calculation.

These three calculations establish that the direction from which the wind was blowing could not have been more than a point off the designation E.N.E. 1/2 N.

This brings us to another dramatic piece of evidence. As the ship drifted west from Clauda, it would have been pointed due north. We know this because it could not have been pointed directly into the wind without capsizing. In other words, it had to have been pointed just off the direction from which the wind was blowing. Using this information, we can calculate with some precision both the direction and rate of the ship's drift to the west.

Ancient records reveal that Egyptian grain ships were the largest vessels of the time, being about the size of an early nineteenth century sailing vessel. This size is implicitly confirmed by Luke's statement that there were 276 people on board.

Since their ship was pointed due north, while the wind was from the northeast, we can roughly calculate the direction of ship's lateral - or sideways - drift. The azimuth, or direction, of the ship's drift from Clauda would have been approximately west eight degrees north. The island of Malta is not directly west of Clauda. *Instead, Malta's bearing from Clauda is exactly west eight degrees north.*

This brings us to yet another piece of evidence. Luke states that it took them fourteen days to drift to Malta. The distance from Clauda to the easternmost point of Malta is 476.6 miles. To calculate the westward rate of drift of their ship, it is necessary to know two things: the size of the ship and the force of the gale. We know the approximate size of the ship and it is possible to establish the mean intensity of the gale. We can then calculate an average rate of drift for Paul's vessel. This calculation reveals an average westward drift of one and one half miles per hour. Thus it would take Paul's ship about thirteen days to drift to Malta. *Luke records that it took them fourteen days.*[14]

Midnight on the Fourteenth Day (Acts 27.27-.32)

If you visit the island of Malta today you will find an inlet that is called St. Paul's Bay. Ancient tradition has hallowed this bay as the site of Paul's shipwreck. The earliest document mentioning this tradition was written more than four hundred years after Paul's shipwreck. However, given the bearing on which their ship was drifting, this bay is the first possible point of contact that they would have had with the island of Malta. Also, there is other evidence that points to this bay as the scene of the shipwreck.

Luke states that at midnight on the fourteenth day the sailors sensed that they were near land. This is a curious statement. Accomplished seamen are sometimes able to smell land while it is far away, but the gale driving them would not have permitted land smells to reach their vessel. It is possible that they dimly heard the sound of waves crashing against the shore, but this must remain a conjecture since Luke does not say why they thought land was nearby.

Interestingly, we have the record of a nineteenth century British court martial that deals with a shipwreck in St. Paul's Bay. The circumstances of the wreck are not quite the same as those found in Acts. While the British ship's approach to the bay was also at night, there was no storm. The shipwreck was caused by the negligence of those on watch. But the general course of the British ship was the same as Paul's vessel eighteen centuries before. Both approached the bay from the east.

For a ship to enter St. Paul's Bay from that direction, it first must pass close to the Point of Koura, which juts out into the surrounding sea. It was at this point that the British lookout was first aware that land was nearby, since he could see the surf crashing against the Point. The gale that was driving Paul's ship would have made the surf even more visible and the breakers would have been heard even before they were seen. Perhaps this is what Luke meant when he said that the sailors "sensed" that land was nearby.[15]

Luke records that, following this, the sailors dropped a line and measured twenty fathoms. A little further on, they dropped the line again and found fifteen fathoms. Now any ship that nears land will first pass over twenty fathoms, then over fifteen, as it closes with the shore. But the route of Paul's ship was more complicated than simply closing with the shore. His vessel was not headed directly toward Malta, but was drifting leeward on a course almost parallel to it.

For the ship to have entered St. Paul's Bay on this course, it would have had to pass within a quarter mile of Koura Point. You can follow the approximate line of the ship's drift on the map of St. Paul's Bay (page 158). Within a quarter mile of passing Koura Point, there is an average depth of twenty fathoms. A little farther west lies the fifteen fathom mark. Again, it needs to be emphasized that these depths are not found on a course that is closing with the island, but on one almost parallel to it.

Luke says that, when the sailors sounded fifteen fathoms, they threw out the anchors because of fear that they would end up on the rocks. You will notice, on the map of St. Paul's Bay, that Salmonetta island is just west of Koura Point, about one quarter mile west of the fifteen fathom mark. This small island is made up of breakers that would not only have been heard at this point, but would have been seen. Their only possible chance for avoiding shipwreck was to try to anchor the ship and halt their drift until morning. At daybreak, they would be able to see whether it was possible to beach the vessel on shore.[16]

An attempt to anchor in the teeth of a gale is always an act of desperation. The anchors of ancient ships were incapable of holding in most bays during a storm. But the bottom of St. Paul's Bay has a clay of unusual characteristics. This is remarked upon in official British navy sailing directions from the nineteenth century. The directions state that anchors in St. Paul's Bay will never pull loose, no matter how bad the storm, because of the local clay. This is an unusual environmental condition.

Luke states that they anchored the ship from the stern. Sailing ships, both ancient and modern, anchor from the front, or prow, since it is impossible to maneuver a ship that is anchored from the stern. But it makes sense that they would anchor from the stern in this case, since the wind would then swing the front of the ship around and point it directly into the bay. In the morning, after looking for the best place to run aground, they could cut the anchors loose and drive the ship onto the beach. If they had anchored from the front of the vessel, with the rear facing toward the shore, they would not have had time to turn the ship around to face the shore and would have capsized.

Luke does not tell us why the anchoring was done from the stern. We discover the reason by analyzing the nautical evidence. Ancient literary sources reveal that this technique of anchoring from the stern was known. Appian reports that Rome won a naval battle against the Carthaginians by using this tactic, their ships suddenly wheeling in unison to meet the enemy. In the nineteenth century, Lord Nelson won the battle of the Nile against the French by this maneuver.[17]

At this point in Luke's narrative, a short drama occurs. Some of the sailors let down the ship's boat under the pretense of laying more anchors, but their real intention is to escape. Some scholars have argued that this episode must be fictional, since it would have been suicide for the sailors to make for an unknown shore at night on stormy seas. The argument is valid – it would have been suicide – but this does not mean that it did not happen. After all, the anchors holding the ship could have given way at any time during the night, or the ship might have begun breaking up under the pounding of the waves. They had been running in a gale for fourteen days, so the ship must have been in very poor condition. An attempt to make for shore may have seemed worth the risk.[18]

The Wreck (Acts 27.33-.44)

At dawn, none of the sailors recognized the coastline. Since Malta's harbor was on the other side of the island, this was understandable. Even sailors who had been to Malta would have had no reason to recognize this particular bay.

Luke records that there was a sandy beach facing them. The modern St. Paul's Bay does not have a sandy beach, but it is geologically possible that there was one two thousand years ago.

In preparation for running aground, the sailors cut the anchor ropes, untied the steering oars, then raised a sail on the prow. These details fit what we know about the handling of ancient ships. There were two steering oars in the stern that acted as rudders. For the ship to have been successfully anchored from the stern the previous night, those oars would have to have been lifted out of the water and lashed together. Luke did not mention that this occurred the night before, but he now reveals that it happened by saying that they untied the oars. The raising of the foresail makes sense, since the mainsail yard-arm had probably long since disappeared in the storm. The small foresail would give the ship some maneuverability.

In verse forty-one, Luke states that the ship ran aground on a sandbank. However, Luke's Greek can be translated in more than one way. It can mean a sandbank, a shallows, or, more literally, "a place of two seas." This last phrase denotes two bodies of water separated by a sandbar. In St. Paul's Bay, there is a narrow inlet of water between Salmonetta island and the Malta mainland. If they ran aground on a sandbank near this inlet, and this is the likeliest place for them to have run aground, it could legitimately be called "a place of two seas."[19]

According to Luke, the front of the ship went aground, but did not break up. It remained intact while the rear gradually disintegrated under the force of the waves. The passengers made their way ashore either by swimming or by floating on pieces of the vessel. Miraculously, there was no loss of life.

This is a very unusual event. For a wooden ship to embed itself in a sandbar without breaking apart, it must run into a mud that will slow it down, then its hull must lodge in a clay tenacious enough to hold it in place. As previously noted, St. Paul's Bay possesses a clay capable of this. However, it is unusual to find mud at the depth of a ship's hull close to a shore. Mud can be found where a creek empties into the sea, but even then it is usually carried away by the current. Only under certain conditions is the water close to shore calm enough for a deposit to form at hull level. As it happens, St. Paul's Bay contains two creeks, as well as the necessary conditions for mud to form near the shoreline.

In short, there are two unusual geological conditions in St. Paul's bay, both of which are necessary for the event that Luke describes.[20]

From Malta to Rome (Acts 28)

Once ashore, they discover that they are on the island of Malta. Because of the cold rain, the inhabitants gather wood and build a fire for them. As Paul is throwing some sticks on the flames, a viper crawls out of the wood and bites him. The Maltans expect him to die. When nothing happens they say that he must be a god.

In modern Malta, there are almost no trees. Nor does the island have poisonous snakes. However, in Paul's time, much of the Mediterranean basin was still wooded. There may also have been poisonous snakes on Malta, although there is no evidence for this apart from the Acts record.[21]

In verse seven, Luke states that they were the guests on Malta of a man named Publius, who was called "the first man of the island." Ancient inscriptions reveal that the head official on Malta had the title "First Man of the Island."[22]

In verse eleven, Luke records that they stayed at Malta for three months before sailing for Italy. There is some disagreement among ancient authorities over when the spring shipping season began. According to Pliny, the Mediterranean was considered open for navigation when the west wind began to blow on February eighth. Vegetius states that the sea lanes were closed until March tenth. In reality, it was probably the weather that dictated the beginning of the sailing season. Paul's vessel wrecked in the first half of November, so three months would have carried them to the middle of February.[23]

Boarding ship at Malta's harbor, they sailed to Syracuse in Sicily, and then to Rhegium in Italy. The following day, a wind began to blow from the south and they made Puteoli in two days. The distance from Rhegium to Puteoli is 230 miles. Sailing before a south wind at 5 knots, they could easily have covered the distance in two days. In the first century, the port of Puteoli was the regular terminus for the Egyptian trade, being the second most important port in Italy after Rome's port of Ostia.[24]

Some scholars have argued that Luke's statement (in verse fourteen) that they stayed with Christians in Puteoli for a week cannot be accurate since Paul was a prisoner and not a tourist. It is true that if they stayed in Puteoli for a week, it could only have been because the Centurion agreed to the delay. He would also have had to agree to Paul's staying with local Christians. How likely is this?

Under the Roman system, the Centurion had the obligation to deliver his prisoners to the authorities in Rome, but possessed complete discretion in what he did with them in the meantime. How and when he got them to Rome was up to him. Since they landed at Puteoli after several days at sea, the Centurion may have wanted to delay the overland trip to Rome.

Because Paul was a Roman citizen, with all the privileges that accompanied that distinction, the Centurion may have wanted to accommodate him. Paul and the Centurion had endured much together over many months. It is not impossible that the Centurion delayed a week in Puteoli.

The delay may even have been necessary if they were waiting for government transport to Rome. They would have been better fed and lodged by local Christians than if they had used local public facilities.

Unlike modern armies, the Roman military had no quartermaster corps to provide food or lodging. The army supported itself by requisition from the local population. Military requisition, even more than taxation, was a cause for complaint and unrest in the empire. Puteoli was a major port for military traffic. Historical records reveal that the inns and boarding houses of Puteoli, and on the road to Rome, were of extremely poor quality during this era. Because these establishments were forced to provide free food and lodging to military and government officials, there was no reason for them to be well maintained. Thus a Christian offer of assistance may have been welcome to the Centurion.[25]

Luke records that, after his arrival in Rome, Paul was kept under house arrest for two years while awaiting trial before the emperor's court. Other ancient authorities confirm that prisoners who appealed to the emperor were sometimes kept waiting for years before their case was tried.[26]

The book of Acts ends at this point, without revealing whether Paul was ever brought to trial. Because the narrative concludes without Paul's being tried, some scholars argue that the book of Acts was probably written during those two years.

According to a tradition that dates to the second century, Paul was tried before the emperor and then released. He went on another missionary journey, this time to Spain. He was then re-arrested and returned to Rome during the first real persecution of the church by the Emperor Nero. It is said that on this occasion Paul died a martyr's death. Such is the tradition. Unfortunately, we possess no contemporary record of these events.[27]

Paul's Evidence

Chapter 6

Paul's Letters to Corinth and Rome

In any attempt to recover the past, it is always useful to possess a contemporary record of events. It is even more useful to have two contemporary records, so that their testimony may be analyzed and compared.

The book of Acts is not the only first century account of Paul's journeys. Although Paul's letters are primarily concerned with matters of theology and church discipline, they also refer in passing to many of the details of his journeys. Unlike Acts, Paul's letters are not written as a narrative of those events. But Paul does provide us with many details about those journeys, so that we are able to compare his account with Luke's.

The evidential relationship between these two sources is a complicated one. Sometimes it is necessary not only to compare a passage in one of Paul's letters to a passage in Acts, but also to passages found in other letters, or to other passages in the same letter. A second problem is that Paul sometimes describes an event in detail that Luke hardly mentions. Taken by itself, Luke's account may imply something that is contradicted by Paul's details. Is there really a contradiction between them, or is it just Luke's brevity that misleads? A third problem is that there are seeming contradictions between the two sources that might be solved if we had more information. Should we consider those contradictions to be proven, or should we assume that if we had more information they would disappear?

These subtle relationships will be explored over the next three chapters. We begin with Paul's letters to Corinth and Rome.

The Chronology of the Letters

These three letters were all written during Paul's third journey. They also reveal the order in which they were written. All three mention a collection of money that Paul is putting together to take to the Christian poor in Jerusalem. In reading the letters, we can follow the progress that Paul is making on this project.

In the first Corinthian letter, Paul instructs the Christians at Corinth to set aside money each week, so that when he comes the collection will be ready to take to Jerusalem.[1] In the second Corinthian letter, Paul tells them that a collection is also being organized by the Macedonian churches, and that he has pointed to the Corinthians as an example to follow. He remarks that they have had their collection ready for over a year.[2] In the Roman letter, Paul states that he is now preparing to leave for Jerusalem with the collection from Christians of Macedonia and Greece.[3] Thus we know that the letters were written in the following order: First Corinthians, Second Corinthians, Romans.

We can also establish the place at which Paul wrote each letter. In the first letter to Corinth, he states that he is writing from Ephesus.[4] In the second letter to Corinth, he says that he is writing from Macedonia.[5] In the Roman letter, Paul does not say where he is writing from, but there is circumstantial evidence that he is writing from Corinth. Several of the individuals named in this letter are associated with Corinth both in Acts and in Paul's other letters.[6]

This sequence of movements – Ephesus, Macedonia and Corinth – corresponds to Luke's description of Paul's third journey. According to Luke, Paul stayed in Ephesus for more than two years, visited Macedonia, and then spent three months in Greece before leaving for Jerusalem.[7]

Is it possible that the author of Acts constructed his narrative based upon a reading of these three letters? Yes, it is possible, but highly unlikely, since he would have to have gone painstakingly through Paul's letters while looking for these particular clues. As we have noted previously, in the ancient world this kind of research was unknown. Historians either wrote from personal experience or reproduced what their immediate sources told them. Thus it is highly unlikely that Acts is dependent on a reading of these three letters. Instead, Paul's letters independently support Luke's account of the chronology of the third journey.

The Jerusalem Collection

Judging from the three letters, the collection of money for the Christian poor of Jerusalem was a major undertaking. Churches from four Roman provinces – Asia, Galatia, Macedonia, and Greece – contributed to the fund, and the collection was in preparation for well over a year. Yet despite the importance of this project, Luke does not mention it in Acts.

Or rather, he does mention it, but in such a way that no one reading Acts alone would guess that this is what he is talking about. According to Acts, in the speech made during his trial in Judea, Paul remarks off-handedly that the reason he returned to Jerusalem is because, "After an absence of several years, I came to bring charitable gifts to my nation and to offer sacrifices."[8]

If nothing else, this passage demonstrates that Acts is independent of Paul's letters. Luke is simply not interested in reporting the Jerusalem collection. The appearance of that collection in the narrative is inadvertent, brought up only to refer to Paul's reasons for returning to Judea. It is not even called a collection for the Christian poor, but is described as a charitable gift for the Jewish people.

Some scholars argue that this demonstrates that Luke was ignorant of the existence of the collection and that he has someone gotten a garbled account of it that he has confused with "gifts to the Jewish nation." But this argument ignores the purpose of Paul's speech in Acts. Paul is making a rhetorical point by identifying himself with the Jewish people. Just as American Jews today might send money to a particular group in Israel and then refer to the donation as "going to Israel," so Paul could legitimately refer to the collection as going to the "Jewish nation," since the Christians in Jerusalem were Jews.[9]

The First Letter to Corinth

We turn now to Paul's first Corinthian letter. In that letter, Paul states that he will not be leaving Ephesus for Macedonia and Greece until after Pentecost, because a great opportunity has opened for the gospel in Ephesus. This is confirmed by Acts, which records that Paul was extremely successful in Ephesus during this period.[10]

This brings us to a second piece of evidence. If Paul had not written a second letter to Corinth, or if that letter had been lost to history, the travel plans that he outlines in the first Corinthian letter would contradict Luke's account of his movements in the third journey.

According to Luke, Paul left Ephesus, spent a short time in Macedonia, and then spent three months in Greece before leaving for Jerusalem following the Passover.[11] In the first Corinthian letter, Paul states he plans to leave Ephesus after *Pentecost* to visit Macedonia and Greece, and then to leave for Jerusalem after the Passover. If he had followed that plan, his visit to Macedonia and Greece would have lasted ten or eleven months, rather than the four or five months recorded in Acts. But since Paul's second

Corinthian letter exists, we know that he changed his plans. He delayed his visit.[12] Thus there is no contradiction between this letter and Acts.

Another important piece of evidence concerns Timothy's movements. In the first Corinthian letter, Paul states that he is sending Timothy to *Corinth* in preparation for Paul's visit to them.[13] However, according to Acts, Paul sent Timothy and Erastus to *Macedonia* in preparation for his visit to Macedonia and Greece.[14]

On the surface, these two passages would seem to be in contradiction. However, since Acts reports that Paul was planning to go to both Macedonia and Greece, it makes sense that Timothy would go to both places, even if Acts does not report that he went on to Greece. At the same time, even though Paul says nothing in his letter about Timothy's going to Macedonia, he does say that he will be visiting Macedonia before coming to Corinth. Again, it makes sense that he would send Timothy to Macedonia as well as to Corinth, even though he does not mention it in the letter.

This conjecture is supported by a curious statement that Paul makes in his letter to Corinth: "If Timothy comes, put him at his ease."[15] *If* Timothy comes? This implies that Timothy might not come to Corinth at all. Though Paul states that he has already sent Timothy to Corinth, clearly he does not expect Timothy to be there when the letter arrives and then adds that Timothy might not arrive at all. So where is Timothy? Paul does not say, but Luke does. Timothy is in Macedonia.

There is additional evidence. In his second letter to Corinth, Paul does not refer to the subject of Timothy's visit with them. But he does include Timothy in the letter's salutation. This means that Timothy was with Paul while he was writing the second Corinthian letter, *and that letter reveals that Paul was in Macedonia on his way to Corinth.*[16]

If we only possessed Paul's letters, and Acts were lost to us, we might assume that Timothy first visited Corinth and then went to

Macedonia to meet Paul. But because we have Acts, we know that Paul sent Timothy to Macedonia, and because Acts does not record that he went on to Greece, *we become aware of the possibility that Timothy never went to Corinth at all.* Since Paul, in the first Corinthian letter, suggests that Timothy might not arrive in Corinth, and in the second letter does not mention Timothy's going there, the probable assumption is that Timothy never arrived. However, it is only when we place Acts and Paul's letters side by side that we discover this.

Apollos

Another evidential relationship involves the Christian evangelist Apollos.

Paul begins his first letter to Corinth by appealing to the Christians in that city to end their divisions. One faction claims to follow Paul, another to follow Peter, another to follow Apollos, while yet another claims to follow Christ alone. Paul emphatically states that factionalism is wrong and argues that they should be united in Christ. Referring to his ministry in Corinth, Paul states: "I planted, Apollos watered, but God gave the increase...."[17] He then states that Apollos is currently at Ephesus.[18]

The book of Acts also mentions Apollos. At the conclusion of his second journey, Paul leaves Aquila and Priscilla in Ephesus while he goes to Jerusalem. During his absence, they convert Apollos. According to Luke, Apollos was an Alexandrian Jew who believed in Jesus as Messiah, but followed some doctrine about him taught by certain followers of John the Baptist. An impressive speaker, Apollos left Ephesus shortly after becoming a Christian and went to Corinth, where he confounded his Jewish opponents in public debate.[19]

In short, both sources connect Apollos to Corinth prior to Paul's writing the first Corinthian letter. They also provide us with an overlapping record of Apollos' movements between Ephesus and Corinth during this period.

Other Evidence from the First Corinthian Letter

In the first Corinthian letter, Paul refers to the fact that he is working for a living while in Ephesus.[20] In the Acts account of Paul's two years in Ephesus, Luke does not record this information. But Luke does record a later speech of Paul's, during which he refers to earning his living while among the Ephesians.[21]

Another coincidence between Acts and this letter concerns the list of people whom Paul says he personally baptized at Corinth. The list is short, as Paul himself emphasizes – Crispus, Gaius, and the family of Stephanas.[22] Since Paul generally did not personally baptize his converts, one might speculate that Paul baptized these individuals because he had a special relationship with them. In the first Corinthian letter, Paul says that the family of Stephanas were his first converts in Greece,[23] while in his letter to Rome, Paul reveals that he is living at the home of Gaius.[24] Both of these passages suggest a personal relationship between Paul and those individuals.

This leaves Crispus. According to Acts, one of the leaders of the Jewish synagogue in Corinth was named Crispus, who became a Christian during Paul's first visit to that city. This was a major event, since it was not every day that a leader in the Jewish community became a believer.[25] In short, a special relationship existed there as well. Paul's personal relationship with the first two individuals is revealed in his letters, while Acts reveals the nature of the third relationship. Once more, the two sources provide overlapping information.

Paul's list of those he baptized does present one problem. In the first Corinthian letter, Paul states that the family of Stephanas were his first converts in Greece. But according to Acts, Paul's first converts were in Athens. Their names were Dionysius and Damaris, together with some other converts who are not named.[26] But this contradiction may be more apparent than real. Corinth and Athens are not far apart. It is possible that Stephanas and his family were among the "others" recorded by Acts in Athens. It is also possible that Paul is generalizing when he calls this family his first converts. His words are "the first fruits of Achaia (Greece)." According to Acts, Paul was only briefly at Athens, then spent a year and a half at Corinth. Even if Stephanas and his family were only the first converts at Corinth, they would still be among "the first fruits" of Greece.

Another piece of evidence concerns a man named Sosthenes. Acts records that, during the first visit to Corinth, Paul was arrested and brought to trial before the Roman Proconsul Gallio. Following Paul's acquittal, the crowd beat Sosthenes, one of the leaders of the Jewish synagogue.[27] It is impossible to tell from Acts whether Sosthenes was a Christian or was simply one of Paul's Jewish opponents. The implication is that he was one of Paul's opponents. On the other hand, since Luke reports the incident as if his readers would be familiar with this individual, perhaps he was a Christian.

The single occasion in which this name appears in Paul's letters is found in the salutation of the first Corinthian letter. Paul and his "colleague Sosthenes" greet the Christians at Corinth.[28] When Paul includes someone's name in a salutation, it generally means that this person was known to the church being addressed. The name Sosthenes was comparatively rare in antiquity. The fact that this name appears once in Acts and once in Paul's letters, and in both cases refers to someone connected with the Corinthian church, probably means that the same individual is being referred to.[29] Again, Luke and Paul overlap in their information.

At the conclusion of the first Corinthian letter, Paul writes that "the churches of Asia salute you."[30] This statement that there were churches throughout the Roman province of Asia is confirmed by Acts, which records that in the two years Paul spent at Ephesus he traveled throughout the province, causing "all who dwelt in Asia to hear the Word."[31]

The Second Letter to Corinth

In the second Corinthian letter, Paul states that he is writing from Macedonia while on his way to Corinth.[32] This means that the letter would have been written shortly after the riot in Ephesus, as recorded in Acts.[33] None of Paul's letters mentions this riot, even though it is a major event in Acts. However, Paul does make this cryptic statement in the second Corinthian letter:

> "We do not want you to be uninformed, brothers, about the hardships we suffered in the province of Asia. We were under great pressure, far beyond our ability to endure, so that we despaired even of life. Indeed, in our hearts we felt the sentence of death. But this happened that we might not rely on ourselves but on God, who raises the dead."[34]

The only similarity between this statement and Luke's account of the Ephesian riot is that, in both cases, Paul was in personal danger. According to Acts, Paul's friends had to restrain him when he attempted to come out of hiding and address the rioting mob. Again, Luke and Paul overlap in their information, but are independent in their testimony.

Strangely, Acts makes no mention of Paul's being persecuted in Ephesus before the riot. However, in the first Corinthian letter, Paul writes of the problems caused by his "many adversaries" there.[35] Actually, Luke refers indirectly to the existence of these "many adversaries." In an account of Paul's speech to the Ephesian elders, delivered on a later occasion, Paul talks about the many problems that he faced during his two years at Ephesus, including "the hard times that came to me because of the plots of the Jews."[36] Notice that the words "plots" is plural. Thus does Acts indirectly

confirm Paul's letter and reveals that Paul faced opposition in
Ephesus even before the riot.

Aid from Macedonia

In the second Corinthian letter, Paul remarks that, on his first
visit to Corinth, he did not depend upon the Corinthians to support
him, but was aided by friends from Macedonia.[37] He repeats this in
a later letter written to the Christians at Philippi, in Macedonia,
when he reminds them that they were the only church who actively
sent help to him.[38]

Acts contains no direct reference to this financial help, but there
is an interesting passage that appears to point to it. Luke records
that when Paul first arrived in Corinth he worked for a living, but
after Timothy and Silas arrived from Macedonia he began
preaching full time.[39] He does not say why Paul stopped working
and started preaching. It is only when we read Paul's letters that we
can guess that financial aid arrived with Timothy and Silas.

It is also possible that representatives from the Macedonian
churches came with Timothy and Silas. Paul's letter refers to "the
brothers who came from Macedonia." Acts, written long after the
event, records only the arrival of Timothy and Silas. Though the
Acts passage makes no mention of anyone else, Christians from
Macedonia may have arrived with Timothy and Silas.[40]

Paul's Sufferings

One of the most dramatic pieces of evidence found in the
second Corinthian letter concerns Paul's description of the various
punishments that he endured in the course of his career. He writes
that he has been whipped by Jewish authorities on five occasions,
flogged by Roman authorities three times, stoned once, and has
been in three shipwrecks.[41]

Most of these events are not recorded in the book of Acts. Luke
states that Paul was stoned at Lystra and records another attempted
stoning. He also states that Paul was flogged by the Roman

authorities at Philippi.[42] The shipwreck narrated in the closing chapters of Acts occurred several years after the second Corinthian letter was written, so the three shipwrecks mentioned by Paul happened before the one narrated by Luke. In short, Acts and the second Corinthian letter agree on only one item found on Paul's list: that Paul was stoned once.

Because of this, it is hard to imagine that the author of Acts was dependent on the second Corinthian letter for information about Paul. Someone writing Acts, with access to this letter, would have wanted to tell us more about Paul's heroism. But Luke consistently narrates Paul's journeys as concisely as possible. Even when he tells us of Paul's sufferings, Luke's accounts are largely devoid of emotion and sentiment. It is only from Paul's own account of his sufferings that we get the full measure of the man.

Some scholars argue that because Paul does not record some of the sufferings chronicled in Acts, this means that Acts is unhistorical.[43] But Paul's list in the second Corinthian letter is not meant to be exhaustive. It was a spontaneous recounting of the things that had happened to him.[44]

Some scholars also argue that Paul's list of sufferings cannot be made to fit into the chronology of Acts. The weakness of this argument is that Luke tells us almost nothing about the years immediately following Paul's conversion, except to say that Paul spent them in his home province of Cilicia. Paul confirms the existence of this period in his Galatian letter, and says he lived fourteen years in Syria and Cilicia following his conversion. This allows enough time for these events to have occurred.[45]

Also, it should be noted that Luke's account of Paul's first two missionary journeys is quite compressed, up to the point that Paul enters Macedonia. Some of the sufferings recorded by Paul could also have happened during the first two journeys.

That Paul should have been involved in three shipwrecks, then later in a fourth while on his way to Rome, seems implausible. But ancient ships were notoriously fragile, and ancient literature is full of personal narratives of shipwreck. Some of the writers of those accounts were also shipwrecked more than once. According to

Acts, at the time that Paul wrote Second Corinthians, he had already been on nine major voyages.[46] How many other voyages Paul made, that are not recorded by Acts, can only be guessed at.

Essentially, this passage shows two things: first, that Acts and Paul's second Corinthian letter are independent of each other, and second, that despite differences in detail, they do not contradict each other.

The Third Visit Problem

According to Acts, Paul made two visits to Corinth. However, the second Corinthian letter reveals a third visit sandwiched between these two. Paul twice states in this letter that he is on his way to visit the Corinthians for the third time (which would be the second visit recorded in Acts).[47] Although it is possible to interpret Paul's Greek so it does not refer to a third visit, the most natural reading is that it does.[48]

There is another passage in Second Corinthians that points to an extra visit. Paul refers to his previous visit to Corinth as painful, because of the internal divisions of that church.[49] This cannot refer to the first visit recorded in Acts, because that is when Paul established the church.[50] But it does fit a visit that might have occurred after the *first* Corinthian letter was written. The main subject of that letter was the divisions within the Corinthian church, and Paul warned them that his coming visit would not be a pleasant one.[51] If, in the first Corinthian letter, Paul was predicting an unpleasant visit, while in the second Corinthian letter we find Paul reflecting back on an unpleasant visit, it is logical to assume that a visit to Corinth has occurred that Acts does not record.

Does the Acts chronology allow time for such a visit? It should be remembered that, in the first Corinthian letter, Paul refers to his coming visit as a general tour of Macedonia and Greece before his return to Jerusalem. But as we have already noted, the second Corinthian letter reveals that this general tour was postponed.[52]

Thus there was time for a short, intervening visit to Corinth. In other words, the second Corinthian letter probably refers to a visit to Corinth that is not recorded in Acts.

Some scholars argue that this proves that Acts is an unreliable history. The problem with this argument is that Acts is a summary of Paul's major movements. It was not written to be a detailed itinerary of Paul's ministry. In Acts, the internal problems of Paul's churches are never mentioned, while Paul's letters are chiefly concerned with those problems. This may be why Acts does not mention Paul's brief visit to Corinth during his years in Ephesus. That visit took place because of the internal problems of the Corinthian church, and Luke was only interested in the larger story.

Titus

In the second Corinthian letter, Paul writes at length about the activities of his close associate Titus.[53] He also refers to Titus in several other letters, including the letter written specifically to Titus.[54] Yet Acts never mentions Titus. At the very least, this omission demonstrates that the author of Acts was not dependent on Paul's letters to write his history. It also demonstrates that the book of Acts does not record everything that Paul ever did, or the name of every one of his associates.

The Letter to Rome

There are a number of details in Acts that are confirmed by the Roman letter. In that letter, Paul states that he has long wanted to visit the church at Rome and that he plans to stop there while on his way to Spain.[55] This passage is paralleled in Acts. During the third journey, Paul says that after he revisits the churches of Macedonia and Greece, "I must also see Rome."[56] While there is no mention of Spain in Acts, this is probably because Paul never made it there. At the end of Acts, Paul was a prisoner in Rome.

Paul also remarks, in the Roman letter, that he has preached the gospel from Jerusalem to Illycrium.[57] This is confirmed by Acts, which records Macedonia as the furthest point west that Paul had preached at this time.[58] Since Illycrium is the next Roman province west of Macedonia, both sources are in agreement, even though they state the matter in different ways.

An interesting psychological divergence exists between the Roman letter and Acts when it comes to Paul's trip to Rome. In his letter, Paul is fully confident that he will soon visit Rome.[59] According to Acts, however, he was apprehensive about the outcome of his visit to Jerusalem and was afraid for the future.[60] Actually, Acts and the Roman letter do not contradict each other because the two accounts do not cover the same time period. In the Roman letter, Paul's confidence that he will soon be in Rome occurs prior to his return journey to Jerusalem, and even in the letter he asks the Roman Christians to pray that his enemies in Judea would not gain the upper hand during his visit.[61] Acts, on other hand, reveals Paul's forebodings only during the course of the return trip to Jerusalem.

Some scholars see a contradiction in the fact that Acts places Aquila and Priscilla with Paul in Ephesus during the third journey, while his Roman letter greets them as living in Rome. However, this seeming contradiction is also a question of timing. Paul spent two years in Ephesus before going to Corinth, which is where the Roman letter was written. Aquila and Priscilla could easily have moved to Rome during that two-year period. Indeed, Acts records that they first met Paul in Corinth during the second journey after being forced to leave Rome. So it is not improbable that they would return to Rome.[62]

One other point needs to be made about Aquila and Priscilla. Paul tells the Christians at Rome that "they risked their necks to save my life." Acts does not record any incident where Aquila and Priscilla risked their lives to save Paul. This is another indication that Luke's history is not based on Paul's letters. It also shows that Acts does not record every event in Paul's life.

Two Lists of Names

Another interesting piece of evidence concerns two lists of names, one found in Acts and one found in the Roman letter. The Acts list contains the names of the men who accompanied Paul on the return trip from Corinth to Jerusalem.[63] The Romans list, which was written by Paul before leaving Corinth for Jerusalem, names some of the individuals who are with him in Corinth who want to send their greetings to the Christians at Rome.[64]

The Roman letter contains eight names, while the Acts list has seven names. What is interesting is that there are only two names common to both lists: Timothy and Sosipater. The name of Timothy, of course, is prominent in both Acts and Paul's letters, but the name Sosipater appears nowhere else in the New Testament. Luke even calls him Sopater, which is the nickname for Sosipater, while Paul calls him by his full name.

Of the remaining five names found in Acts, three appear in letters that Paul later wrote while in prison: Trophimus, Aristarchus, and Tychicus.[65] According to Acts, Trophimus was the proximate cause of Paul's arrest in Jerusalem, while Aristarchus accompanied Paul on the voyage to Rome.[66] Tychicus is mentioned on four occasions in Paul's prison letters, but this is his only appearance in Acts.[67] In short, the three men whom Acts lists as accompanying Paul to Jerusalem also ended up, according to Paul, with him in Rome. Finally, there are two names on Luke's list that appear nowhere else in the New Testament: Secundus and Gaius the Doberian.

These details provide a kind of subtle evidence. If the eight individuals Paul names in his letter had simply been listed by Luke as accompanying Paul to Jerusalem, we would strongly suspect that Luke had copied those names from Paul's letter. But only two of the names appear on both lists. In the case of one name, Sopater, this is his only appearance in the New Testament. Further, three of the individuals that Acts records as accompanying Paul to

Jerusalem are named in Paul's later letters as being with him in Rome. In all these details, we have a confirmation of names that is both coincidental and indirect.

This concludes our study of Paul's Corinthian and Roman letters. In general, we see a minute and subtle relationship between these letters and the book of Acts. The details that Paul relates about his movements, as well as about the movements of his associates, overlap and confirm what Luke has to say about those events. At the same time, it is clear that each is writing without reference to the other source.

Chapter 7

Paul's Galatian Letter

One of the few serious arguments against the historical accuracy of Acts can be made in relation to Paul's Galatian letter.[1] On the surface, at least, these two sources appear to contain a number of historical details that cannot be reconciled.

Part of the problem lies in the fact that the events they record took place early in Paul's career. The Galatian letter was probably written within two years of those events, and it refers to them in some detail. Acts, on the other hand, was written at least sixteen years later and deals with these events only in passing. However, even taking this into account, there are real difficulties in reconciling these two records.

There are two major problems. First, in Galatians 2, Paul describes a meeting with the Apostles on the circumcision issue in the church. Acts 15 also describes a meeting that Paul had with the Apostles on this issue, but the account of that meeting is quite different. Second, in Galatians, Paul describes his movements in the immediate days, months, and years following his conversion. There are a number of difficulties in reconciling his account with the details found in the book of Acts.

Galatians 2 and Acts 15

*In Galatians 2, Paul reports on a private meeting with the
Apostles. During this meeting, certain Jewish Christians insist that
Titus, Paul's gentile assistant, be circumcised in accordance with
Jewish religious law. However, the Apostles side with Paul when
he refuses to do this. In Acts 15, Luke tells of a public meeting
called by the Apostles to decide the circumcision issue for the
church. The result of the meeting is a public declaration that
gentile Christians do not have to be circumcised.*

Both of these passages report a meeting that Paul had with the
Apostles. However, if they are reporting on the same event, they
are in dramatic contradiction. Paul's letter records a private
meeting during which the issue of his gentile assistant is raised.
Acts records a public meeting called specifically to settle the issue
of gentile circumcision for the church.

Those scholars who defend Luke's account argue that the event
recorded by Paul in Galatians 2 is not the meeting of Acts 15. They
also argue that the private meeting of Galatians 2 probably took
place during an earlier visit that Paul made to Jerusalem, the visit
described in Acts 11.30. In other words, they find no contradiction
between Galatians 2 and Acts 15 because those passages refer to
different events.

Is this a reasonable explanation, or is it more reasonable to
believe that Galatians 2 and Acts 15 refer to the same event? In
fact, there are weighty and persuasive arguments on both sides of
this question. Let us call the argument for identifying Galatians 2
with Acts 15 the argument of the prosecution, and the argument for
identifying Galatians 2 with Acts 11.30 the argument of the
defense.

Prosecution Arguments and Defense Replies

1) Prosecution: In Galatians 2 and Acts 15, Paul and Barnabas
travel from Antioch to Jerusalem for a meeting with the Apostles.

Although Paul and Barnabas travel to Jerusalem in Acts 11.30, no meeting with Apostles is recorded.

Defense: While there is no mention of a meeting with the Apostles in Acts 11.30, it should be remembered that Paul states that he met with the Apostles privately on this occasion. Luke is primarily concerned with recording public events. Thus it makes sense that Acts 11.30 does not record that meeting.

2) Prosecution: In both Galatians 2 and Acts 15, gentile Christians accompany Paul and Barnabas from Antioch to Jerusalem. This does not occur in Acts 11.30.

Defense: While no gentile Christians are mentioned in Acts 11.30 as accompanying Paul and Barnabas to Jerusalem, they could have done so without Luke's mentioning that fact. Paul and Barnabas went to Jerusalem as representatives of the church at Antioch, which was largely made up of gentile Christians.

3) Prosecution: In both Galatians 2 and Acts 15, the people involved in the meeting are the same: Paul, Barnabas, James, Peter, and some unnamed Jewish Christian critics of Paul. Paul and Barnabas alone appear in Acts 11.30.

Defense: Luke, in this brief passage, does not produce a list of names of people who were in Jerusalem. But Luke elsewhere implies that James and Peter were resident in Jerusalem during this period, while from the time that Peter baptized the first gentile convert until the meeting of Acts 15, there were Jewish Christian critics of the gentile mission in Jerusalem. In short, it is reasonable to believe that James, Peter, and Paul's critics were all present in Jerusalem at the time of Acts 11.30.

4) Prosecution: In both Galatians 2 and Acts 15, the meeting settled the theological question of whether gentile Christians had to be circumcised. In both cases, the Apostles side with Paul and Barnabas. This important issue would have been decided by the Apostles only *once*. Thus Galatians 2 and Acts 15 *must* refer to the same meeting.

Defense: The prosecution misinterprets Galatians 2. A close reading reveals that the circumcision issue was not the reason for Paul's meeting with the Apostles and that the meeting did not settle the issue. What Paul actually says is that, during his private meeting with the Apostles, he was confronted by some Jewish Christians who demanded that he circumcise his gentile assistant Titus. Paul says that he refused to do so and that the Apostles backed him up.

This is completely different from the event recorded in Acts 15. In that case, the circumcision controversy was the stated reason for the meeting with the Apostles. The meeting was public and was called to settle the matter for the whole church. At the end of the meeting, a public document was issued by the Apostles. These crucial details prove that the identification of Galatians 2 with Acts 15 is wrong. It is two different meetings that are being referred to.

Prosecution (reply): Yes, we agree that Galatians 2 and Acts 15 contradict each other in their main details. This is because Luke, or his sources, have reproduced a garbled and romantic account of what occurred at that meeting. Paul's letter records the actual event.

Defense (reply): The prosecution is going beyond the evidence in making this argument. It is more reasonable to assume that Galatians 2 and Acts 15 refer to two different meetings, than that they refer to the same meeting, but that Luke has got all the details wrong. Acts 11.30 represents the most probable date for the private meeting described in Galatians 2.

5) Prosecution: There is other evidence for the identification of Galatians 2 with Acts 15. For example, the Galatian letter must have been written by Paul *after* meeting of Acts 15, thus his references must be to that meeting. We know that the Galatian letter was written after the events of Acts 15, because there is simply not enough time for Paul to have written it before that event.

Let us examine Luke's timetable. According to Luke, after the first journey to Galatia, Paul stayed only a short time in Antioch before leaving for the Jerusalem meeting of Acts 15. In other words, during that short period, his Jewish opponents had to enter Galatia, persuade his converts to their theological position, the news of these events had to get back to Paul, and he had to write the Galatian letter. There is not enough time for all of these events to have happened.

Defense: There is enough time. In Acts 15.33, Luke records that Paul stayed "some time" with the church at Antioch. "Some time" could, in fact, mean many months. Once this is understood, the prosecution's argument loses much of its force. Note that Paul, in the Galatian letter, expresses his surprise at how *swiftly* the Galatians have defected from his teaching. Thus Paul himself reveals that the amount of time involved cannot have been very great. The Galatian letter could have been written before the Council of Acts 15.

6) Prosecution: During the Council of Acts 15, the Apostles agree upon a letter to be sent to the gentile churches. This letter is addressed to the churches of Syria and Cilicia, but not to the churches of Galatia. However, Luke has Paul taking the letter to the Galatians on the second journey.[2] Here is more evidence of Luke's historical confusion. The letter he references was not sent to the Galatians at all, but to the churches of Syria and Cilicia. The letter that Luke reproduces as being distributed to the Galatians had nothing to do with the Galatian church.

Defense: We agree that it is odd that the Apostolic decree was addressed only to Syria and Cilicia. However, this is hardly decisive evidence. There are several possible explanations for why the letter was not addressed to the Galatian churches.

First, the letter reproduced by Luke may have been a copy of the letter that was sent to the churches of Syria and Cilicia. Another similar letter may have been sent to the churches of Galatia.

Second, because it was the church at Antioch that sent Paul and Barnabas to Jerusalem, it may be that the Apostles' letter was formally addressed to the churches in the province of which Antioch was the chief city (Syria, with Cilicia as a dependency).

Although the formal reply was to the Syrian church, since they had raised the question, the letter would apply to all gentile churches.

Third, because the churches of Galatia were established by Paul and Barnabas as missionaries from the church at Antioch, it is possible that they were considered to be an extension of the Syrian church. In that case, the Galatian churches would be included in a letter addressed to Syria and Cilicia.

7) Prosecution: In Galatians 1.18, Paul states that, three years after his conversion, he went up to Jerusalem from Damascus. Then, in Galatians 2.1, he states that, fourteen years later, he went up to Jerusalem again for the meeting with the Apostles.

This is a total of seventeen years. This fact *alone* proves that the identification of Galatians 2 with Acts 11.30 is wrong. Again, let's look at Luke's timetable. If Jesus' resurrection was in 30 AD and Paul's conversion was in 33 AD, seventeen years after this would 50 AD. According to the defense theory, this is when the meeting of Acts 11.30 took place. But this is far too late a date. This is the year that Claudius expelled the Jews from Rome and is one year before Gallio became Proconsul of Corinth. Both of these events took place at the time of Paul's second journey. This means that, in the course of a single year, Paul had to go on the first missionary journey, engage in the Council of Acts 15, then go on the second missionary journey. It is impossible for all of these events to have occurred in the space of one year.

Defense: We agree with the prosecution that this is impossible, if there were *seventeen* years between Paul's conversion and the meeting of Acts 11.30. But it is possible that Paul is not referring to a total of seventeen years. We argue that the three years following Paul's conversion are meant to be understood as running *concurrently* with the fourteen years during which Paul was in Syria and Cilicia. In that case, there would be a total of fourteen years. We grant that the most natural reading of Paul's statement is that he meant a total of seventeen years. But it is possible to read the passage as meaning fourteen years.[3]

Defense Arguments and Prosecution Replies

Now we turn to arguments from the defense, with replies from the prosecution:

1) Defense: There are a number of details that prove that the meeting of Galatians 2 cannot be the meeting of Acts 15. In Galatians, circumcision comes up during the course of the meeting, while in Acts it is the reason why the meeting was called. In Galatians, Paul states that he met with the Apostles privately, while in Acts there is a public meeting with a publicly announced decision at the end. In Galatians, Paul plays a major role in the meeting, while in Acts Paul is in the background and the Apostles take center stage. In Galatians, Paul does not refer to the Apostles' letter to the gentile churches, while in Acts the letter and its public distribution are central to the outcome of the meeting. These are two different meetings being described.

Prosecution: All that this shows is that Luke, or his sources, have unhistorically turned the private meeting of Galatians 2 into the public meeting of Acts 15, and have added details that are contradicted by Paul's own record. While historical evidence points to the fact that the Apostles did issue some kind of letter to the gentile churches, it was probably issued on a later occasion. The fact that it was issued to the Syrian churches shows that it had nothing to do with the Galatians. Luke simply includes the letter in his erroneous account of Paul's meeting with the Apostles.

2) Defense: In the Galatian letter, Paul reveals that his private meeting with the Apostles was only the second time that he had met with them following his conversion. He says that, following his conversion, he traveled to Jerusalem and met with the Apostles, then spent fourteen years in the regions of Syria and Cilicia. He then again returned to Jerusalem for the meeting of Galatians 2.

This exactly what Luke records. Luke says that Paul visited Jerusalem following his conversion, then went to his home city of Tarsus, in Cilicia, for a number of years. He next visited Jerusalem in Acts 11.30. This is decisive evidence that the meeting of Galatians 2 took place during the Jerusalem visit recorded in Acts 11.30.

Prosecution: It is only on the surface that this appears to be decisive evidence. In Galatians, Paul is not referring to *every* visit that he made to Jerusalem following his conversion, but only to the number of times that he met with the *Apostles*. We reiterate our main point, which is that Acts 11.30 does not mention a meeting with the Apostles. Paul met with them once after his conversion and again *seventeen* years later. This is the meeting of Acts 15.

3) Defense: In his Galatian letter, Paul records an incident involving Peter that took place following Paul's Galatian 2 meeting with the Apostles. Peter visits the church at Antioch and freely associates with the gentile Christians. But after the arrival of "some men from James,"[4] Peter withdrew from all contact with the gentiles, much to Paul's disgust.

Under Jewish religious law, Jews were forbidden to associate with uncircumcised gentiles. If, as the prosecution contends, the meeting of Galatians 2 settled the circumcision issue, then Peter's actions make no sense. However, they do make sense if they followed the private meeting described in Galatians 2, which dealt only with the circumcising of Paul's gentile assistant. A permanent settlement of the circumcision issue had to wait until the meeting of Acts 15.

Prosecution: There are two possible replies to this evidence. First, Galatians 2 may have settled the circumcision issue *without* settling the issue of Jewish-gentile association in the church. Theologically, they are distinct issues. Second, Paul often writes parenthetically in his letters and jumps from one event to another without regard to chronological order. It is possible that the incident in Antioch occurred *before* Paul's meeting with the

Apostles, although the most natural reading of Paul's letter points to it happening after that meeting.

4) Defense: According to Acts 11.28, it was the prophet Agabus' prophecy of a famine that prompted the Christians in Antioch to send assistance to the Christians of Judea. This was the reason for the Acts 11.30 visit to Jerusalem. In Galatians 2.2, Paul states that he went to Jerusalem in response to a revelation. This fits the reason given for his visit in Acts 11.30, but does not fit the visit of Acts 15. Paul also states, in Galatians 2.10, that after the meeting the Apostles urged him to continue to remember the poor. Since it is Acts 11.30 that records Paul and Barnabas bringing assistance to the poor of Jerusalem, the Apostles' statement that Paul should "continue" to remember the poor fits the visit of Acts 11.30, but not the visit of Acts 15.

Prosecution: The defense goes beyond the evidence in making this argument. Paul does state in Galatians that a revelation prompted him to go to Jerusalem. However, he does not say what that revelation was. The defense assumes that it was Agabus' prophecy, but it could have been some other revelation. Second, the fact that the Apostles urged Paul to *continue* to remember the poor is a statement that could have been made on any occasion. It is not necessarily tied to the events of Acts 11.30. Indeed, there is a difference between people who need famine relief and people who are simply poor.

This concludes our review of the arguments that surround this much controverted question. The fundamental issue is whether we are required to believe that Paul's account in Galatians 2 refers to the meeting of Acts 15. If it does, then Luke and Paul are in radical disagreement over the details of that meeting. But if Galatians 2 refers to the Jerusalem visit of Acts 11.30, then there are no essential contradictions between the two sources.

At a minimum, the defense has established that the similarities between Galatians 2 and Acts 15 also exist – as a possibility –

between Galatians 2 and Acts 11.30. The prosecution, on the other hand, while demonstrating that there *may* exist contradictions of detail between Acts 11.30 and Galatians 2, does not finally *prove* that those contradictions exist.

In short, the prosecution has failed to prove that Galatians 2 must refer to the meeting of Acts 15, while the defense has established that Galatians 2 may refer to the events of Acts 11.30. Beyond these tentative conclusions it is not possible to go.

Paul's Conversion

The second major problem in reconciling Galatians with Acts concerns the events immediately following Paul's conversion.[5] On the surface, Paul's description, in the Galatian letter, of those events contradicts the Acts account. Again, we will present the prosecution arguments and the defense replies:

1) Prosecution: Paul states, in Galatians, that he consulted with no one after his encounter with Christ, but "immediately" departed for Arabia, afterward returning to Damascus. According to Acts, however, Paul spent the next three days in Damascus, sightless and fasting. Then Ananias, a local Christian, came to heal Paul and to baptize him. Afterward, Paul stayed on in Damascus, preaching and teaching, until he was forced to leave for Jerusalem. Acts does not even mention a visit to Arabia and also keeps Paul in Damascus for at least three days after his conversion. This contradicts Paul's clear statements in the Galatian letter. [6]

Defense: Acts consistently records Paul's major movements and ignores his minor ones. The Galatian letter implies that the Arabian visit was quite short, so it is reasonable to believe that Luke omitted it because it plays no role in the larger narrative. As for Paul's statement in Galatians that he left for Arabia "immediately" following his conversion, it is reasonable to believe that immediately could mean three days later. People often say that they did something "immediately," but then it turns out that they did a few other things first.

2) Prosecution: Acts records that Paul consulted with Ananias, although in the Galatian letters Paul claims to have consulted with no one before going to Arabia.[7]

Defense: Acts does not record that Paul "consulted" with Ananias. Ananias only came to heal and baptize him. When reading Paul's statement in Galatians, it is necessary to recall the context. Paul is trying to establish that he received his commission as an Apostle directly from Christ and was under the authority of no other Apostle. Ananias was not an Apostle nor does Acts portray Paul as being under his authority.

3) Prosecution: Paul states that he stayed in Damascus for three years before returning to Jerusalem. But according to Acts 9.23, Paul's stay in Damascus was only "many days." This is a direct contradiction of fact.

Defense: The real question is whether it is possible that the phrase "many days" can mean "three years." We submit that it can. In the ancient world, years were reckoned inclusively. Thus if Paul arrived in Damascus in one calendar year and left in a third calendar year, he would be reckoned as staying in Damascus for three years, even if he had been there for a little over a year. Acts itself provides an example of this kind of reckoning. In Acts 20.31, Luke quotes Paul as saying that he lived in Ephesus for three years, while in Acts 19.8 Luke states that Paul was resident there for two years and three months. "Many days" is an indefinite period of time. It may very well mean more than a year, just as "three years" may mean just a little over one year.

4) Prosecution: There is other evidence that Luke regarded Paul's stay in Damascus as being quite short. According to Acts, the disciples were afraid of Paul when he arrived in Jerusalem after his conversion. They simply could not believe that their former persecutor had become a Christian. The problem is that this passage makes sense only if Paul's conversion were recent. It makes no sense if there were a year or more between his

conversion and his return to Jerusalem. By then, it would be old news. What this proves is that Luke believed that Paul stayed only a short time in Damascus.

Acts also records that, when Barnabas introduced Paul to the Apostles, he referred to Paul's conversion as if it were a recent event. Again, this proves that Luke thought that Paul stayed only briefly in Damascus.[8]

Defense: The church in Jerusalem had been under intense persecution for several years. For them to hear at a distance that their chief persecutor had suddenly come over to their side was one thing, but for the man himself to appear, after a long absence, may have prompted caution on their part.

Another possibility is that they feared Paul because of the hatred directed toward him by the Jews. Although the church at Jerusalem had faced persecution at the hands of their fellow Jews, they had recently reached an accommodation with them. Paul, on the other hand, was involved in directly confronting the Jews in Damascus, which is why he was driven out of that city. The Jerusalem church may have felt themselves to be in danger, not from Paul, but from being associated with him.

As for Barnabas' introduction of Paul to the Apostles, a close examination of this passage shows it to be a formal statement about Paul's history, and not a comment about his recent past.

5) Prosecution: In Galatians, Paul states that during his visit in Jerusalem he met with Peter and stayed with him for fifteen days. He writes that he saw none of the other Apostles, except for James the Lord's brother. According to Acts, however, Paul met with "the Apostles" on this visit. The implication is that he met with all of the Apostles. Of course, it can be argued that Peter and James constitute two "Apostles," so that Acts is technically correct. But the implication remains that Paul met with the Apostles as a group.

It should also be noted that Acts never refers to James as an Apostle. Luke, in both his gospel and in Acts, consistently calls the twelve *disciples* Apostles, and James was not one of the twelve. So, even technically, Paul did not meet with the "Apostles."

Defense: It is difficult to reconcile Paul's statement that he saw only Peter and James with Luke's claim that he met with "the Apostles." It can be argued that Peter and James constitute more than one Apostle, but as the prosecution notes there are difficulties even with this argument. However, in contradiction to the prosecution's claim that Luke refers only to the twelve as Apostles, it should be noted that Acts also calls Paul and Barnabas Apostles. So it may simply be an oversight that Luke never refers to James as one.

Still, the defense concedes that Luke may have committed an error in this passage, though it is not a particularly important one. Writing more than two decades after the event, Luke may be generalizing from the information that he possesses, and so refers to a meeting with the "Apostles," even though Paul met only with Peter and James.

The North Galatian Hypothesis

There is one other problem in reconciling Galatians and Acts. Some scholars argue that there is sufficient internal evidence in the Galatian letter to prove that it was written to Christians in the northern part of Galatia. However, Acts records that Paul and Barnabas started churches only in the southern part of that province. Further, Acts allows no time for the planting of churches in northern Galatia. Thus this evidence, if conclusive, would demonstrate that Acts is a flawed historical source.

The problem is that the "North Galatian" hypothesis rests largely on speculative evidence. Because that evidence is complex, and because it is not persuasive, those arguments will not be dealt with here. Instead, the interested reader is referred to sources that examine this question.[9] Here we will simply note that there is no substantive evidence that the Galatian letter was written to northern Galatia.

Conclusion

This completes our review of the problems associated with the Galatian letter. Of the contradictions that may have been proven by the prosecution, none are important. Of the prosecution arguments that allege serious contradictions, none are proven.

Still, the problem remains. In the rest of Paul's letters, we have little difficulty in reconciling his version of events with Luke's. Why does the Galatian letter present us with so many difficulties? Doesn't the fact that we have so many problems in reconciling Acts with Galatians call into question Luke's historical reliability?

Actually, the large number of problems does not, by itself, call Luke's accuracy into question. It is often the case, when dealing with independent sources, that discrepancies arise, not because of underlying errors, but because of the nature of the sources themselves. In the Galatian letter, Paul is detailed in what he says. He is also probably writing just two years after the events that he is describing. Acts was written almost two decades later and covers these events briefly, without much detail. Given this reality, it would be surprising if there were no problems in reconciling Acts with Galatians.

Indeed, Acts and Galatians agree in most details. Here is a brief list of the things that they have in common:

1) Paul was a leader among the Jews while still a young man and zealous for the cause of Judaism.[10]
2) Paul savagely persecuted the church.[11]
3) Paul was converted in Damascus.[12]
4) Following his conversion, Paul traveled from Damascus to Jerusalem, then on to the region of Syria and Cilicia, where he spent a number of years.[13]
5) Paul and Barnabas were both resident in Antioch in the early years.[14]

6) Barnabas accompanied Paul on trips from Antioch to Jerusalem.[15]
7) Barnabas was well-known to the Galatians.[16]
8) Barnabas and Paul were a missionary team whose purpose was to convert gentiles.[17]
9) Paul and Barnabas had serious disagreements, although the earlier disagreement recorded in Galatians is not fatal to their relationship, while the later disagreement recorded in Acts is.[18]
10) Paul's opponents were mainly Jews, rather than pagans, during this early period.[19]
11) The first missionary journey to Galatia is immediately, and spectacularly, successful.[20]
12) Paul performed miracles in Galatia.[21]
13) Peter and John stand out from the other Apostles as the central figures of the early church, with Peter the leader and making missionary journeys of his own.[22]
14) James, the brother of Christ, plays a prominent role in the early church.[23]
15) There are gentile churches outside Judea at an early date.[24]
16) The Judean churches hold to the practice of the Jewish religious law, while the largely gentile churches outside Judea do not follow those practices.[25]
17) Jerusalem is the center of the early church and the Apostles are headquartered there.[26]

This completes our review of the evidential relationship between Galatians and Acts.

Chapter 8

Paul's Other Letters

Paul's remaining letters consist of two letters to Thessalonica and his prison letters. The Thessalonica letters were written during the second journey, while the prison letters were probably written either during one of Paul's imprisonments in Rome or during his imprisonment in Caesarea, prior to his appeal to Rome.

Paul's Letters to Thessalonica

The first letter to Thessalonica is written in the names of Paul, Silas and Timothy.[1] According to Acts, all three men were in Thessalonica during the second journey, so all three would be known to the Christians there.[2] This is a minor detail, but it shows that Acts and Paul's letter agree that all three men had been in Thessalonica at this time. Acts also reveals that Silas and Timothy were with Paul in Corinth when the first letter to Thessalonica was written.[3]

In the course of the letter, Paul writes that they were "shamefully treated" at Philippi before coming to Thessalonica. This mysterious statement is all that Paul says about a matter that is dealt with in detail by Luke in his account of Paul's illegal beating and jailing by the magistrates of Philippi.[4]

Paul also states that they had been unwillingly separated from the Thessalonian Christians, suffering persecution in the process. Again, Paul gives no details, but Acts reveals that Paul and his associates were forced to leave Thessalonica because of a riot caused by his opponents.[5] Once again, Paul refers to an event while Luke provides us with the details.

Paul records some events in this letter that do not appear in Acts. He tells the Thessalonians that he has unsuccessfully attempted to re-visit them more than once since fleeing Thessalonica. He states that he will soon make another attempt to see them.[6] Acts records no attempted visits to Thessalonica during this period, or any visits to Thessalonica prior to the third journey.[7] It is possible that Paul briefly re-visited the Thessalonians during the year and a half that he spent in Corinth, but if he did Acts does not tell us about it.

A more complicated question concerns the movements of Paul's associates during this period. On the surface, Acts and the first Thessalonian letter would seem to contradict each other. In the letter, Paul states that "we" decided to stay on alone in Athens and that he had sent Timothy back to Thessalonica. Then Timothy returned (probably after Paul had gone to Corinth).[8] According to Acts, on the other hand, Silas and Timothy stayed in Berea and did not accompany Paul to Athens. Instead, Paul went with unnamed "others." Paul then sent the "others" back to Berea to tell Silas and Timothy to join him, and they were re-united with him after he left Athens and arrived in Corinth.[9]

In reality, the details from these two sources fit together quite nicely once it is understood that Luke is only giving a bare outline of these movements. Here is a possible chronology that reconciles the two sources:[10]

> 1) Paul leaves Silas and Timothy in Berea while he goes to Athens. After arriving, he immediately sends for them. (Acts 17.14-.16)

2) Silas and Timothy join him in Athens.
(Supposition)

3) Paul then sends Timothy to Thessalonica.
(1 Thess. 3.1-.2)

4) Paul also sends Silas to Thessalonica or
elsewhere in Macedonia. (Supposition)

5) After a short stay in Athens, Paul goes to
Corinth. (Acts 18.1)

6) Paul is joined in Corinth by Timothy and
Silas who are returning from Macedonia. (Acts
18.5 and 1 Thess. 3.6)

6) Paul writes the Thessalonian letters from
Corinth.

While this reconstruction of events is speculative, it is a
reasonable explanation for the seeming contradiction between the
two sources. One of the rules of evidence that we are following is
that a contradiction cannot be proved if there is a reasonable
explanation for it. This chronology is a reasonable explanation for
this seeming contradiction. It assumes that everything that Luke
and Paul tells us is true, but that Luke has not given us complete
information. If it is reasonable to assume this, the alleged
contradiction is not proved.

There are several other evidential correspondences between the
first letter to Thessalonica and Acts:

1) Paul states that the Thessalonians have suffered persecution
from their own countrymen. This remark is confirmed by the Acts
account of the riot at Thessalonica, which was the work of local

gentiles although instigated by Paul's Jewish opponents.[11] In the cities that Paul visited, Acts does not always record that recent converts were persecuted by the pagan population of that city. In this case, both Acts and the first Thessalonian letter agree that the Thessalonians were persecuted by their fellow citizens.

2) According to Acts, Paul arrived in Thessalonica, spent three Sabbaths in the synagogue arguing with the Jews, and then a riot broke out and he was forced to leave the city.[12] In reading this passage, the natural conclusion is that Paul stayed in Thessalonica for about three or four weeks.

But Paul's first Thessalonian letter, as well his letter to the Philippians, imply a longer period of time. In the Thessalonian letter, Paul writes: "Surely you remember, brothers, our toil and hardship; we worked night and day in order not to be a burden to anyone while we preached the gospel of God to you." This implies a longer period.[13] In the Philippian letter, Paul seems to say that the Philippians sent him monetary assistance twice while he was in Thessalonica, which is improbable if he were only there for a few weeks. Actually, Paul's Greek could as easily mean that they sent him assistance while he was in Thessalonica and then again on some other occasion. So this passage does not necessarily prove that Paul received assistance twice while in Thessalonica.[14]

If we had nothing but Paul's letters to Thessalonica and Philippi, we would think that Paul had spent an extended period in Thessalonica. But Acts implies that it was a matter of weeks. Ultimately, these sources can be reconciled because Paul's letters do not actually require us to believe that he was there for a longer period of time.

3) Another seeming contradiction between Acts and the first Thessalonian letter is found in Paul's statement that the Thessalonian Christians had turned from idols to serve God. Paul writes throughout the Thessalonian letter as if most of those whom he is addressing were converted from idolatry. However Acts

records that Paul's converts in Thessalonica consisted mainly of Jews and God-fearing gentiles associated with the Jewish synagogue. None of these people had been idolaters.[15]

But if Luke has made an error here, it is not a severe one. It may be that Luke has oversimplified what occurred at Thessalonica. Or it may be that he rightly named the group of people whom Paul initially converted, Jews and their gentile proselytes, and that later additions to the church – after Paul left Thessalonica – were mainly made up of former pagans. In that case, there would not be a contradiction between the two sources. Instead, Luke would simply be telling us about the those who became believers during Paul's initial visit to Thessalonica.

This brings us to Paul's second letter to Thessalonica. In this letter, there are no important evidential correspondences with Acts, except yet another reference to Paul's working for a living while among them.[16]

Paul's Prison Letters

All of Paul's prison letters were probably written during one of his imprisonments in Rome. Some scholars have argued that some of the letters were written during his two year imprisonment in Caesarea, prior to the voyage to Rome, or even during a possible earlier imprisonment in Ephesus. However, from the standpoint of the evidential relationship between Acts and Paul's letters, it makes no real difference if this is true. Further, it should be noted that there is no substantive evidence that any of Paul's prison letters were written earlier.[17]

The Letters to Philippi and Colossae

Most of the evidence contained in Paul's letter to the Philippians has already been noted. In addition, the letter to the Philippians contains a brief remark in which Paul exhorts them to suffer for Christ's sake, just as they saw Paul himself suffer while he was among them. This brief aside, where Paul provides no details about what happened to him, is confirmed by Luke's account of Paul's illegal flogging and imprisonment while in Philippi.[18]

In the Colossian letter, Paul names three men who are currently with him, one of whom is Aristarchus.[19] According to Acts, Aristarchus was one of two Christians dragged into the theater at Ephesus by the rioting crowd.[20] Since the city of Colossae was near Ephesus, it makes sense that Aristarchus would be known to the Christians there and that Paul would refer to him in the Colossian letter. Acts also states that Aristarchus accompanied Paul on the voyage to Rome.[21] Since the Colossian letter was probably written from Rome, this demonstrates yet another factual agreement between the two sources.

The second name on Paul's list, Mark, also appears in Acts. But Acts records a very short-lived relationship between them. Mark was to have accompanied Paul and Barnabas on the first missionary journey, but turned back at the very beginning of that journey. When they set out on the second journey, Barnabas wanted to take Mark with them again, but Paul refused to have him. This caused the breakup of Paul and Barnabas' partnership and they never worked together again. Acts never mentions Mark again.[22] If Acts were the only source that we had, we would assume that Paul, Barnabas and Mark were permanently estranged from one another.

However, the Colossian letter – as well as two other of Paul's prison letters (Philemon and second Timothy) – depicts Mark as a close associate of Paul's during his imprisonment.[23] Paul does not reveal in his letters that Mark was the reason that he and Barnabas had ended their collaboration many years before. But the Colossian letter does reveal a possible motive for Barnabas' insistence that Mark accompany them on the second journey. Paul refers in passing to the fact that Mark is Barnabas' cousin.[24] It is only when we take the information contained in Acts about Mark, and put it together with the information in Paul's letters, that we get a full picture of who Mark was and what role he played in the history of Paul's journeys.

The third Christian named by Paul in the Colossian letter is Jesus Justus. This name does not appear anywhere else in the New Testament. We know nothing at all about this individual except that Paul includes him in his greetings to the Christians at Colossae.

The Letters to Timothy and Titus

According to tradition, Paul's letters to Timothy and Titus were written after he was released from his first Roman imprisonment. According to that tradition, Paul journeyed to Spain, then was re-arrested and sent back to Rome. This time he perished during the first real persecution of the church by the Emperor Nero.

This tradition, although dating to the second century, has no substantive evidential support. However, the letters that Paul wrote to Timothy and Titus contain details about various individuals and their movements that cannot be reconciled with Acts' account of Paul's journeys. Either Acts contains substantial errors or the events that these letters record took place after the events narrated in Acts.

If we suppose that these letters were written after the completion of Acts, then the first letter to Timothy and the letter to Titus would have been written during Paul's short period of freedom before his re-arrest. The second letter to Timothy would have been written during Paul's second Roman imprisonment. This letter reveals that Paul expected to be executed at any moment.[25]

There is one possible conflict between these letters and Acts. According to Acts, Paul informed the Ephesian elders at Miletus, at the end of his third journey, that they would never see him again. He had a premonition that something would happen to him after his return to Jerusalem. However, the two letters to Timothy reveal that he visited the Ephesian church one final time. This was probably following his first Roman imprisonment.[26]

Now if Paul is expected to be infallible in his premonitions, these passages contradict Luke's statement that Paul expected never to return to Ephesus. But if infallibility is not predicated of Paul, there is no contradiction. To the contrary, this evidence establishes that the author of Acts had no knowledge of Paul's later visit to Ephesus. If Acts were written during Paul's first Roman imprisonment, as some scholars suppose, then this visit to Ephesus would not yet have occurred.

In the second letter to Timothy, Paul remarks on the faith of Timothy's mother and grandmother, and on the fact that Timothy has known the scriptures since childhood. In all of Paul's references to Timothy in his letters, this is the only hint we have that Timothy was Jewish. Acts states that Timothy's mother was Jewish and goes on to say that his father was a gentile.[27]

Paul also reminds Timothy of the persecutions that he endured in Antioch, Iconium and Lystra. These three cities are all located in the same region as Derbe, which Acts records as the only other city that Paul visited in that region. Acts records that, of these four cities, Derbe was the only city in which Paul did not face persecution. So Acts and Paul are in agreement. Paul was persecuted in all the cities in that area, except for Derbe.[28]

Paul also asks Timothy to recall to his mind the experience of those early persecutions. This means that Paul was acquainted with Timothy during the first missionary journey. But Timothy's name does not appear in Acts until Paul's stopover in that region during the *second journey*. At that time, Timothy signed on as one of Paul's associates. However, there is no real contradiction here. Acts does not say that Paul and Timothy first met on the second journey, but only that Timothy joined Paul's missionary enterprise on that occasion. Indeed, the fact that Timothy joined Paul during Paul's brief stopover in Derbe during the second journey indicates that they were previously acquainted. The two sources overlap in their information.[29]

With regard to Paul's letter to Titus, it has already been pointed out, in the chapter on Paul's letters to Corinth and Rome, that Titus' name does not appear in Acts. Even though Titus was a close associate of Paul's, and his name appears on a number of occasions in Paul's letters, Acts does not mention him. Once again, Acts does not tell us everything about Paul.[30]

In his letter to Titus, Paul quotes from the pagan poet Epimenides. Acts also has Paul quoting from Epimenides, during his appearance before the Areopagus in Athens. Even though Acts does not know the name of Titus, both Acts and the letter to Titus reveal Paul's interest in this ancient poet.[31]

This concludes the evidence from Paul's prison letters. The evidence reveals that Acts and these letters are independent sources narrating a common history. Paul's version of events serves to demonstrate the underlying accuracy of the Acts narrative.

Conclusion

By now, the reader should have a solid grasp of the historical evidence surrounding the record of Paul's journeys. However, there are still a few pieces of evidence that we have not yet touched upon. This remaining evidence deals with the book of Acts as a whole, rather than being tied to particular passages. Briefly, that evidence can be summarized as follows:

1. Who was the Author of Acts? [1]

According to tradition, Luke wrote both Acts and the gospel that bears his name. This tradition can be traced to the middle of the second century AD, but there is no other evidence that clearly identifies Luke as the author of these books.

Luke is mentioned only briefly in the New Testament. Although his name is not found in Acts or in Luke, this is not surprising, since ancient historians generally did not refer to themselves in their writings. His name does appear in three of Paul's letters: Colossians, Second Timothy, and Philemon. Paul tells us three things about Luke: that he was one of Paul's associates, that he was a gentile, and that he was a doctor.

From linguistic evidence, we know that it is almost certain that the same individual wrote both Luke and Acts. There is an extremely close similarity of language and style in these two works. There is also the author's claim, in Acts 1.1, that he is writing a continuation of his gospel, and Luke and Acts are both addressed to the same individual, Theophilus.

Some scholars maintain that Luke and Acts show a familiarity with medical terms that is not found in the other writings of the New Testament. Because Paul states that Luke was a doctor, this would seem to point to Luke as the author of Luke-Acts. However, other scholars argue that any well-educated writer in the ancient world could have used those particular terms.

While it can be said that Luke and Acts contain more medical terms than any other book of the New Testament, this does not, by itself, prove that a doctor wrote Luke and Acts. On the other hand, if doctor wrote these two books, it would be surprising if these terms were not used.

2. What were Luke's Sources in Writing Acts? [2]

The book of Acts is the second longest book in the New Testament and covers a period of more than thirty years. The narrative begins with Jesus' resurrection (circa 30 AD) and ends with Paul as a prisoner in Rome (circa 62 AD).

Most of Acts is written in the third person. It seems clear that the author of Acts was not a personal witness to most of the events that he describes. So the question arises as to what sources he relied upon in writing Acts, and whether those sources can be discovered by a close examination of the narrative.

Although some scholars claim to have isolated Luke's sources, such reconstructions are highly theoretical. There is no hard evidence pointing to the sources that Luke used; there are only inspired guesses based on the prominence of certain individuals and places in the text.

There are four passages in the second half of Acts where the author speaks as if he were present at events. In those verses, he stops writing in the third person plural and begins writing in the first person plural. We know, from the example of other ancient writers, that when an author writes in the first person plural he is generally claiming to be an eye-witness to the events that he is describing. So we should probably conclude that the author of Acts is making the same claim.

It is worth noting that the amount, and vividness, of Luke's narrative detail increases as we near the end of Acts. Paul's first journey is told in bare outline. Paul's second and third journeys are described in more detail, especially after he crosses the Aegean to Macedonia and Greece. The account of Paul's Judean arrest and trial is full of description, while the short narrative of the voyage and shipwreck contains many details. Clearly, the author of Acts is more interested in later events than he is in earlier events. And he is most interested in describing those events in which he took part.

3. What was the Date of the Writing of Acts? [3]

None of the writings of the New Testament are dated. Some scholars attempt to date Acts in relation to a supposed dating of the gospels and Paul's letters, but such dating is a matter of subjective theory. There is no real evidence.

Acts ends with the statement that Paul remained a prisoner in Rome for two years while awaiting trial. Because the author leaves the narrative hanging there, some historians argue that Acts was written before Paul came to trial. This argument has weight, but lacks final proof.

One thing is certain. As has been emphasized throughout this study, the historical details found in Acts reflect the political, social, and legal life of the middle of the first century. It is almost impossible that someone writing Acts at a later date could have discovered those by doing historical research.

As we have noted more than once, the ancients were simply not interested in doing that kind of research. The details that appear in Acts are either the result of the author's personal experience or are derived from his immediate sources. Although the date at which the book of Acts was written must remain unknown, it cannot have been many years after the events that Acts describes.

4. What is the Relationship of Acts to Other Writings? [4]

To understand the literary character of Acts, it is first necessary to understand the nature of literature in the first century. It is only by reading the histories, the fiction writing, and the mythologies from that era that we can come to understand the literary genre to which Acts belongs.

What that study reveals is that Acts is a work of ancient history. It does not resemble a first century work of fiction or a mythology. The only decisive difference between Acts and other ancient histories is that it records miracles, including the miracle of Jesus' resurrection from the dead.

David A. Aune, a specialist in ancient literature, describes it this way: "Luke-Acts is a popular 'general history' written by an amateur Hellenistic historian with credentials in Greek rhetoric...Using his rhetorical skills, Luke adapted the genre of general history, one of the more eclectic genres of antiquity, as an appropriate literary vehicle for depicting the origins and development of Christianity."[5]

5. What is the Relationship of Paul's Theology to Acts? [6]

Paul's letters are largely concerned with theological matters, while Acts is a narrative of events. However, Acts also contains theological statements, many of which are attributed to Paul. Some scholars argue that Paul's theology, as found in his letters, cannot possibly be reconciled with the description of that theology in Acts. They argue that this proves that the writer of Acts was not a companion of Paul.

The nature of Luke's theology, and its relation not only to the writings of Paul, but to the rest of the New Testament, is a problem that requires a book-length study. For the reader who is interested in this question, the relevant sources are provided in the notes for this chapter. Here a summary judgment will be rendered, based on a reading of the experts in the field, that while there are differences in theological understanding between Luke and Paul, none of those differences are decisive. Acts could have been written by a companion of Paul.

As I. Howard Marshall, an Acts scholar, aptly concludes: "This is not to say that there are no points of tension between Luke's portrait of Paul and his own writings; it is to affirm that in our opinion they are not so substantial as to make us dismiss Acts as unhistorical."[7]

Concluding Evidential Postscript

The present study has been concerned with the problem of empirical evidence and its relationship to the record of Paul's journeys.

This stands in marked contrast with the purpose of modern biblical scholarship, which is largely concerned with theoretical matters rather than with evidence. Nor should it surprise us that scholars find theory more interesting than evidence. After all, the primary purpose in getting a Ph.D., or for publishing scholarly papers, is to demonstrate the depth of one's knowledge and erudition. Since the empirical evidence surrounding Paul's journeys is limited and can be understood even by non-scholars, career-track biblical scholarship almost has to be about something else. And that something else must be complex enough so that only the cognoscenti can understand it. As a discipline, biblical scholarship inevitably points away from empirical evidence and toward intellectual novelty.

It does not help that the primary purpose of the New Testament is to record God's intervention in human history. Modern scholarship in general proceeds from an intellectual culture of unbelief. That culture is based on the *a priori* assumption that any theory, no matter how subjective, automatically trumps any argument, no matter how empirical, that points to the possibility of divine intervention in history.

In this study, we have dealt solely with the problem of empirical evidence. Subjective theory has been banned as an historical explanation. Briefly, the empirical evidence can be summarized as follows:

1) Geographical Evidence

Over a period of twenty years, Paul traveled several thousand miles through Judea, Syria, Cyprus, Asia Minor, Macedonia, Greece, Malta, and Italy. Many of his travels were by ship through the Aegean and the Mediterranean seas. Of the dozens of geographical details related by Acts, almost all are accurate. Even the few details that can be questioned are likely to be accurate. Luke's reliability when it comes to geography is astonishing. Ancient writers did not have almanacs or reference guides to consult when writing about highways, shipping routes, provinces, or cities. They wrote what they knew or what their immediate sources told them. Luke and his sources reach a high standard of geographical accuracy.

2) Topographical Evidence

Luke describes the local topography of a number of cities and places in the eastern half of the Roman empire. In each case, the descriptions match what we know about the physical layout of those locations.

3) Archeological Evidence

Modern archeology throws a great deal of light on the reliability of the Acts narrative. Indeed, some of the archeological confirmations of Luke's narrative are spectacular, such as the discovery that Gallio was indeed Proconsul of Corinth in the year that Paul was on trial before him in that city. There is also the discovery of the pavement laid by Erastus, treasurer of the city of Corinth, who may be the Erastus mentioned in both Acts and Paul's letters. There are a number of archeological findings that confirm the Acts narrative, and none which contradict it.

4) Meteorological Evidence

One of the more fascinating areas of evidence concerns the wind and weather described in Acts. This evidence is the most striking in relation to the account of Paul's voyage and shipwreck. That storm must have occurred just as Luke records it, since his narrative fits all the meteorological data. Meteorological data also play a role in verifying other passages in Acts. Whether Paul and his companions are sailing in the Aegean, or along the Mediterranean coast, Luke's record of the number of days that it took to sail to a particular location, at a particular time of year, inevitably corresponds to the meteorological evidence.

5) Nautical Evidence

As more than one commentator has pointed out, the author of Acts is no sailor. Yet this renders Luke's description of nautical events all the more convincing, since he is not writing from knowledge, but from experience. Many of his nautical details are implied in the text. For example, Luke never refers to the current running along the coast of Asia Minor, or the curvature of the coast of southern Crete, or even to the changing directions of the wind.

Instead, all of these details are contained implicitly in his description of events. We discover them because they fit the nautical data contained in his descriptions of the ship's maneuvers and difficulties.

6) Contemporary Evidence

One of the most striking aspects of the Acts record is how many of its political and social details belong to the middle of the first century, and to that era alone. Nor is it just the number of mid-first century details that is impressive, but the fact that these details reflect the very different political and social realities found in the different Roman provinces and cities. There are dozens of these details in Acts and they are all historically accurate.

Whether Luke is dealing with the nature of Roman citizenship and its legal ramifications, with the political boundaries of *regios* within a Roman province, or with the political authority of self-governing cities, his narrative belongs to the middle of the first century and reflects no other period.

7) Legal Evidence

The author of Acts is nearly always reliable in portraying Paul's legal problems, whether those problems reflect local, provincial or imperial law. One might almost think that Acts was written by a lawyer, rather than by doctor. Further, Luke's legal details invariably belong to the middle of the first century. As A. N. Sherwin-White, one of the leading experts on ancient Roman law, points out in his book, *Roman Society and Roman Law in the New Testament*, Luke's account of Paul's legal troubles is a perfect fit with historical reality.

8) Bibliographical Evidence

Very few Christians named in the New Testament are mentioned in contemporary pagan or Jewish writings that have survived the rigors of time. Josephus, Tacitus, and Suetonius refer briefly to Christ and his followers. But other than a smattering of references in other first century writings, this is all the direct information that we have from pagan or Jewish sources.

However, Luke refers by name to a number of pagans and Jews who appear in contemporary pagan and Jewish writings. For example, in his account of Paul's Judean trial, we find several individuals who are written about in non-Christian sources. The movements and activities of these people, as recorded by Luke, are confirmed by those sources.

9) Paul's Evidence

In dealing with the history of Paul's journeys, we are fortunate to possess two independent sources that record the details of those journeys. Acts is a narrative history, while Paul's letters refer in passing to many of the events of the journeys. In general, it can be said that Paul confirms what Luke writes. Often, he provides additional details. Sometimes it is only when the two sources are compared that we discover additional details, which appear only as the result of that comparison.

This does not mean that there are no problems in reconciling Paul's letters and Acts. But a summary judgment of the alleged contradictions between them shows that most of these contradictions cannot be proved, while the remainder are relatively unimportant. In the final analysis, the many indirect agreements between Paul's letters and Acts are so minute, and so detailed, that they establish the historical reliability of Acts on an even firmer foundation.

Although the book of Acts was written almost two thousand years ago, it contains hundreds of circumstantial details that can be confirmed by independent evidence. While the name of Paul, and the details of his journeys, can be found in no first century document outside the New Testament, it is almost certain that Luke's account of Paul's journeys is historically true. The book of

Acts contains too many assertions that have been proven to be true to believe otherwise.

The Acts account of Paul's journeys is as reliable as we may expect history to be. So far as it can be tested by objective evidence, Acts has proven to be an astonishingly accurate record of events.

Notes

The authors and page numbers below are keyed to the books and journals listed in the Bibliography.

Prologue: The Problem of Evidence

1. Gasque 109-110, 248-249, Hemer 329-333
2. Linnemann 111

Chapter 1: The First Journey

1. Sailing to Salamis: Ramsay (1897) 70-72
2. Elymas the Magician: Bruce (1954) 472, Hanson 140, Marshall (1980) 218-219
3. Sergius Paulus: Elderen 151-156, Hemer 109, 166, Nobbs 282-287
4. Pisidian Antioch: Bruce (1951) 260, Hemer 228, Marshall (1980) 222-223
5. The Archisynagogi: Bruce (1951) 260, Marshall (1980) 222-223

6. The Status of Women: Ramsay (1897) 102, Witherington (1988) 5-16
7. The Officials of Iconium: Sherwin-White 78
8. Roman Lycaonia: Bruce (1954) 288, Harnack (1909) 93-94, Ramsay (1897) 102-104, 110-112, Ramsay (1915) 35-63
9. Salvation as a Pagan Term: Ramsay (1915) 173-190
10. The Language of Lystra: Hemer 110, 117
11. Zeus and Hermes: Hansen 393-394, Marshall (1980) 236-237
12. James the Brother of Jesus: Bruce (1951) 296
13. James' Speech: Bauckham 452-462, Longenecker (1975) 87-89
14. The Jerusalem Council's List of Prohibitions: Bauckham 462-467, Bruce (1951) 299, Hanson 155-156

Chapter 2: The Second Journey

1. Jewish Intermarriage in Central Turkey: Ramsay (1915) 353-369
2 .The Connection Between Lystra and Iconium: Hemer 111-112, Ramsay (1897) 178-180
3. Luke's Geography / Lystra to Troas: French 55-58, Marshall (1980) 261-263, Ramsay (1897) 178-179, 194-195
4. Mysia: Harnack (1909) 98, Ramsay (1897) 196
5. Geography/Sailing Time From Troas to Philippi: Bruce (1951) 312, Ramsay (1897) 205-206
6. Philippi and the First District: Bruce (1951) 312, Hanson 169, Sherwin-White 93-94
7. Lydia - the Woman and the Place: Bruce (1951) 314, Ramsay (1897) 213-215
8. The Philippian Charges Against Paul and Silas: Sherwin-White 78-82, Ramsay (1897) 218-219
9. Paul and Silas' Silence About Their Roman Citizenship: Rapske (*Custody*, 1994) 129-134, Sherwin-White 78-82
10. The Earthquake and the Jailer: Marshall (1980) 271-274, Ramsay (1897) 220-222, Rapske (*Custody*, 1994) 202-204, 391-392
11. The Lictors: Sherwin-White 74-75, 97-98
12. First Century Citizenship: Sherwin-White 71-73, 172-174
13. "Beaten without trial": Rapske (*Custody*, 1994) 300-302, Sherwin-White 71-76, 172-173

14. The Power of Civil Expulsion: Sherwin-White 77, 98
15. The Geography from Philippi to Thessalonica: Bruce (1951) 324
16. Thessalonicans are called Greeks: Ramsay (1897) 227
17. The Leading Women of Thessalonica and Berea: Ramsay (1897) 227, 232-233, Witherington (1988) 5-16
18. Politarchs / Thessalonica Self-Governing: Horsely 419-431, Sherwin-White 96
19. Jason's Bond: Sherwin-White 95
20. Athenian Idols / Marketplace: Gill (Achaia, 1994) 443-445, Ramsay (1897) 238
21. The Areopagus: Cadbury 51-52, Ramsay (1897) 246-248, 260-261, Ramsay (1915) 103-105
22. Religiosity of the Athenians: Hanson 175, Thompson 391
23. Statue to the Unknown God: Deissman 287-288, Thompson 391
24. Paul's Areopagus Speech Literary Quotes: Hemer 118, Marshall (1980) 288-289
25. Damaris: Bruce (1954) 364, Ramsay (1897) 252
26. Claudius Expulsion of the Jews / Chrestus: Bruce (1954) 368, Clarke 469-471, Hemer 167-168
27. Paul the Tentmaker: Bruce (1951) 343, Hock 21-23, Rapske (*Custody*, 1994) 106-107
28. Gallio: Hanson 9, 185, Hemer 251-253, Marshall (1980) 297-299
29. The Charge Against Paul in Corinth: Sherwin-White 99-104, Winter (1994) 98-103

Chapter 3: The Third Journey

1. The Lecture Hall of Tyrannus: Bruce (1951) 356
2. Paul's Head-coverings and Aprons: Bruce (1951) 357, Trebilco (1994) 312-314
3. The Jewish Magicians of Ephesus: Bruce (1951) 358-360, Hanson 192, Marshall (1980) 310-312
4. Erastus: Bruce (1982) 280, Cadbury 55, Gill (Acts, 1994) 112, Hemer 235
5. Demetrius and the Shrinemakers: Cadbury 5-6, Sherwin-White 90-92, Trebilco (1994) 336-342

6. "Great is Artemis" / The Theater in Ephesus: Bruce (1951) 364-365, Ramsay (1897) 279, Trebilco (1994) 318-319
7. Asiarchs: Cadbury 42, Kearsly 363-376, Sherwin-White 89-90
8. The People's Clerk: Bruce (1951) 367, Cadbury 41, Sherwin-White 86
9. The Citizen Assembly of Ephesus: Bruce (1951) 365-366, Hanson 198, Sherwin-White 83-88
10. Parallels to the Clerk's Speech / Municipal Riots: Cadbury 84, Sherwin-White 83-86, Trebilco (1994) 344-347
11. Ephesus as "Warden of the Temple": Bruce (1951) 367, Trebilco (1994) 326-336
12. The Meteorite: Bruce (1951) 367, Hemer 122, Hanson 197-198
13. Plural Proconsuls in Asia: Bruce (1951) 368
14. The Trip from Philippi to Caesarea: Hemer 125, Marshall (1980) 327, Ramsay (1897) 291-299
15. Elders and Bishops as the Same Office: Hanson 204
16. Philip's Daughters: Bruce (1951) 387

Chapter 4: Paul's Judean Arrest and Trial

1. Paul's Nazirite Vow: Bruce (1951) 394-395, Hanson 210-211, Marshall (1980) 344-347
2. Penalties for Violating the Temple: Bruce (1951) 395
3. Roman Troops in Jerusalem/Fortress of Antonia: Bruce (1951) 396-397, Rapske (*Custody*, 1994) 137-138
4. The Egyptian Prophet: Bruce (1951) 398, Hanson 9-10, Marshall (1980) 351-352
5. Paul's Identification with Tarsus: Rapske (*Custody*, 1994) 75-83, Sherwin-White 178-180
6. Gamaliel as Paul's Teacher: Marshall (1980) 354
7. The Tribune's Citizenship: Cadbury 74, 79, Rapske (*Custody*, 1994) 143-145, Sherwin-White 154-156
8. Ananias the High Priest: Bruce (1951) 409, Marshall (1980) 362-364, Ramsay (1915) 90
9. Informal Meeting of the Sanhedrin: Ramsay (1915) 90, Sherwin-White 54

10. Pharisees vs. the Saducees: Bruce (1951) 411, Marshall (1980) 364-365, Rapske (*Custody*, 1994) 103
11. Paul's Roman Escort to Caesarea: Hanson 223, Hengel (1995) 64-67, Marshall (1980) 372, Rapske (*Custody*, 1994) 153-154, Rapske (Shipwreck, 1994) 11-14
12. The Tribune's Letter: Sherwin-White 48, 54-55, Winter (1993) 308-309
13. Overview of Roman Judicial Procedure: Sherwin-White 28-31, 48-70
14. Paul's Province and Felix's Response: Rapske (*Custody*, 1994) 155, Sherwin-White 28-31, 55-57
15. Charges Made by the Sanhedrin's Attorney/Paul's Response: Rapske (*Custody*, 1994) 158-163, Sherwin-White 14-15, 48-70, Winter (1993) 335-336
16. Adjournment until the Arrival of the Tribune: Sherwin-White 53
17. Drusilla: Bruce (1951) 427
18. Felix and Bribes: Hanson 230
19. Porcius Festus Becomes Procurator / Felix' Indictment: Bruce (1951) 428-429, Rapske (*Custody*, 1994) 321
20. Two Years Under Arrest in Caesarea: Hemer 173, Rapske (*Custody*, 1994) 317-323
21. Felix and Pallas: Bruce (1951) 428
22. Paul's Appeal to the Emperor: Bruce (1951) 431-432, Rapske (*Custody*, 1994) 186-189, Sherwin-White 57-70
23. Agrippa and Bernice: Bruce (1951) 433-34, Hemer 173
24. People and Events in these Chapters: Hanson 8
25. The Sanhedrin and the Power of Capital Punishment: Hanson 238, Sherwin-White 32-47

Chapter 5: Paul's Voyage to Rome and Shipwreck

1. The Augustan Cohort: Hemer 132, Marshall (1980) 403, Rapske (*Custody*, 1994) 267-270
2. Luke and Aristarchus Accompany Paul: Ramsay (1897) 315-316
3. Caesarea to Myra: Ramsay (1897) 314-318, Smith 61-73
4. The Eygptian Grain Ship: Hemer 149-150, Ramsay (1897) 318-320, Rapske (Shipwreck, 1994) 29-35

5. Myra to Fair Havens: Hanson 244, Hemer 134-135, Ramsay (1897) 320-321, Smith 74-85

6. Day of Atonement / Lateness of the Sailing Season: Bruce (1951) 455, Ramsay (1897) 322, Rapske (Shipwreck, 1994) 22-29

7. Roman Control of Private Shipping: Bruce (1951) 456, Hemer 138, Ramsay (1897) 323-325, Rapske (*Custody*, 1994) 376-378

8. Imperial Inducement to Sail Late in the Season: Rapske (Shipwreck, 1994) 22-27

9. Location of Phoenix's Harbor: Hemer 139, Ogilvie 308-314

10. Fair Havens to Cape Matala: Smith 97-98

11. Euraquilo: Hemer 141-142, Ramsay (1897) 326-328

12. Rigging the Ship Behind Clauda: Hemer 142-144, Ramsay (1897) 328-330, Smith 105-113

13. The Adria: Bruce (1951) 462

14. Drifting 14 Days in the Storm: Hemer 145, Rapske (Shipwreck, 1994) 39-40, Smith 97-128

15. The Sailors "Sense" that They are Near Land: Bruce (1951) 462-463, Smith 120-124

16. Twenty Fathoms followed by Ffifteen: Hemer 147, Smith 129-131

17. Anchoring from the Stern: Smith 131-136

18. Attempted Desertion of the Sailors: Hemer 147-148, Marshall (1980) 412-413

19. "Place of Two Seas": Hemer 150, Smith 140-143

20. Wrecking on the Sandbank: Hemer 150-151, Marshall (1980) 414-415, Ramsay (1897) 340-341, Smith 143-144

21. Vipers and Wood on Malta: Hemer 153, Ramsay (1897) 342-343

22. First Man of the Island: Ramsay (1897) 342-343

23. The Number of Months Spent on Malta / Early Sailing to Italy: Bruce (1951) 455-456, 473, Rapske (Shipwreck, 1994) 22-25

24. Rhegium to Puteoli: Hanson 253

25. Puteoli and the Week's Stay: Marshall (1980) 419, Rapske (*Custody*, 1994) 273-276

26. Paul's Two Year Wait for Trial by the Emperor: Sherwin-White 108-119

27. Paul's Release, Visit to Spain, Re-arrest, and Execution: Ellis 661

Chapter 6: Paul's Letters to Corinth and Rome

1. 1 Cor. 16.1-.4
2. 2 Cor. 8-9
3. Rm. 15.25-.29
4. 1 Cor. 15.32, 16.5-.9
5. 2 Cor. 2.12-.13, 7.5, 9.1-.5
6. Gutherie 396-397 / Paley 23-26
7. Acts 19.10, 20.1-.3
8. Acts 24.17
9. Paley 15-22
10. 1 Cor. 16.5-.9 / Acts 19.1-.41
11. Acts 20.1-.4
12. 2 Cor. 1.15-.23
13. 1 Cor. 4.17, 16.10
14. Acts 19.21-.22
15. 1 Cor. 16.10
16. 2 Cor. 1.1, 2.12-.13, 7.5, 9.1-.5
17. 1 Cor. 1.12, 3.6
18. 1 Cor. 16.12
19. Acts 18.24-19.1
20. 1 Cor. 4.11-.12
21. Acts 20.34
22. 1 Cor. 1.14-.17
23. 1 Cor. 16.15
24. Rm. 16.23
25. Acts 18.7-.8
26. 1 Cor. 16.15 / Acts 17.34
27. Acts 18.17
28. 1 Cor. 1.1
29. Lake and Cadbury 228
30. 1 Cor. 16.19
31. Acts 19.10
32. 2 Cor. 2.12-.14, 7.5, 9.1-.2
33. Acts 19.23-.41

34. 2 Cor. 1.8-.9 (Quote from the New International Version)

35. 1 Cor. 16.8-.9

36. Acts 20.19

37. 2 Cor. 11.9

38. Phil. 4.15

39. Acts 18.1-.5

40. 2 Cor. 1.19

41. 2 Cor. 11.24-.25

42. Acts 14.19, 14.5-.6, 16.22

43. Hughes 405-407

44. 2 Cor. 10-11

45. Acts 9.26-.30, 11.19-.30 / Gal. 1.13-.21

46. Hughes 410-411

47. 2 Cor. 12.14, 13.1-.2

48. Hughes 31-33, 459-462, 473-477 / Lake (1911)145-151

49. 2 Cor. 2.1

50. Acts 18.1-.18

51. 1 Cor. 4.21, 11.34

52. 2 Cor. 1.15-.23 / 1 Cor. 16.5-.9

53. 2 Cor. 2.13, 7.5-.16, 8.6-.24, 12.18

54. Gal. 2.3-.5 / 2 Tim. 4.10 / Titus

55. Rm. 1.13, 15.23-.24

56. Acts 19.21

57. Rm. 15.19

58. Acts 20.2

59. Rm. 15.17-.28

60. Acts 20.18-.23, 21.4, 21.11

61. Rm. 15.31

62. Paley 26-34

63. Acts 20.4

64. Rm. 16.21-.23

65. 2 Tim. 4.12, 4.20 / Col. 4.7-.10 / Eph. 6.21 / Philem. .24 / Titus
    3.12

66. Acts 21.29, 27.2

67. Titus 3.12 / Eph. 6.21 / Col. 4.7-.9 / 2 Tim. 4.12

Chapter 7: Paul's Galatian Letter

1. This chapter is largely based on the work of the following scholars: Emmet 265-297; Gutherie 450-471; Lake (1911) 253-316; Lake (1933) 188-212; Ridderbos 13-36, 75-92; Witherington (1998) 13-20.
2. Acts 16.4
3. Hemer 261-270 / Trebilco (1993) 454
4. Gal. 2.11-.14
5. Gal. 1.17-.18 / Acts 9.1-.27
6. Gal. 1.16-.17 / Acts 9.8-.26
7. Gal. 1.16 / Acts 9.17-.19
8. Acts 9.26-.27
9. Gutherie 450-457; Hansen 378-379; Hemer 277-307; Longenecker (1990) lxii-lxxii; Ramsay (1900); Ridderbos 22-30
10. Gal. 1.13-.14 / Acts 7.58-8.3, 9.1-.2, 22.3
11. Gal. 1.13 / Acts 7.58-8.3, 9.1-.2
12. Gal. 1.17 / Acts 9.3-.6
13. Gal. 1.17-.21 / Acts 9.22-.30, 11.19-.26
14. Gal. 2.11 / Acts 11.25-.30, 13.1-.3, 14.26-15.2
15. Gal. 2.1 / Acts 11.30, 15
16. Gal. 2.1, 2.9, 2.13 / Acts 13-14
17. Gal. 2.1, 2.9 / Acts 11.22, 13-15
18. Gal. 2.11-.14 / Acts 15.36-.40
19. Gal. 5.2-.12, 6.11-.18 / Acts 13.50, 14.1-.2, 14.19, 17.5
20. Gal. 4.12-.14 / Acts 13-14
21. Gal. 3.5 / Acts 14.3
22. Gal. 1.18, 2.7-.11, / Acts 2.37, 3.1, 8.14-.25, 9.32-10.48
23. Gal. 2.9, 2.12 / Acts 12.17, 15.6-.29
24. Gal. 1.2, 2.11/ Acts 9.31
25. Gal. 2.12-.14 / Acts 15, 21.20
26. Gal. 1.17-.18, 2.1 / Acts 8.1, 15.2

Chapter 8: Paul's Other Letters

1. 1 Thess. 1.1
2. Acts 15.40-16.3, 17.5, 17.14-.16
3. Acts 18.1-.5 / 1 Thess. 2.18-3.6
4. Acts 16.11-.40 / 1 Thess. 2.2
5. Acts 17.5-.10 / 1 Thess. 2.17 / 3.4
6. 1 Thess. 2.18, 3.6-.11
7. Acts 17-20
8. 1 Thess. 3.1-.6
9. Acts 17.14-.15, 18.1-.5
10. Lake (1911) 74
11. 1 Thess. 2.14-.16 / Acts 17.1-.10
12. Acts 17.1-.10
13. 1 Thess. 2.9 (Quote from New International Version)
14. Phil. 4.16 / Martin 182
15. 1 Thess. 1.9 / Acts 17.4
16. 2 Thess. 3.7-.9
17. Duncan 66-159 / Gutherie 472-478
18. Acts 16.20-.40 / Phil. 1.29-.30
19. Col. 4.10
20. Acts 19.29
21. Acts 20.4, 27.2
22. Acts 12.25, 13.5, 13.13, 15.35-.41
23. Philemon .24 / 2 Tim. 4.11
24. Col. 4.10
25. 2 Tim. 4.6-.8 / Ellis 661-662 / Paley 257-275
26. Acts 20.25, .38 / 1 Tim. 1.3 / 2 Tim. 4.20 / Paley 269-275
27. 2 Tim. 1.5, 3.14-.15 / Acts 16.1
28. 2 Tim. 3.10-.11 / Acts 13.14-14.24
29. 2 Tim. 3.10-.11/ Acts 16.1
30. Gal. 2.1-.3 / 2 Cor. 2.13, 7.5-.16, 8, 12.18 / 2 Tim. 4.10 / Titus
31. Titus 1.12 / Acts 17.28 / Hemer 186-187

Conclusion

1. The Author of Acts: Bruce (1951) 2-9, Harnack (1907) 12-19
2. Luke's Sources in Acts: Bruce (1951) 21-26, Dupont, Hemer 308-364
3. The Date of the Writing of Acts: Bruce (1951) 10-14, Harnack (1909) 19-20, 295-296, Hemer 365-410
4. The Relationship of Acts to Other Writings: Aune 77-157, Hemer 30-99, Hengel (1979) 15-36, Palmer 1-29
5. David Aune Quote: Aune 77
6. Paul's Theology and Acts: Bruce (1951) 34-36, Hemer 245-247, Marshall (1998)
7. I. H. Marshall Quote: Marshall (1980) 43

Bibliography

Aune, D. E. *The New Testament in Its Literary Environment.*
Philadelphia: The Westminster Press, 1987.

Bauckham, R. "James and the Jerusalem Church." In R. Bauckham,
ed., *The Book of Acts in Its Palestinian Setting.* Grand Rapids, MI:
Wm. B. Eerdmans, 1995.

Bruce, F. F. *The Acts of the Apostles.* Grand Rapids, MI: Wm. B.
Eerdmans, 1951.

Bruce, F. F. *Commentary on The Book of Acts.* Grand Rapids, MI:
Wm. B.Eerdmans, 1954.

Bruce, F. F. *The Epistle of Paul to the Romans.* Grand Rapids, MI:
Wm. B. Eerdmans, 1982.

Cadbury, H. J. *The Book of Acts in History.* New York: Harper, 1955.

Clarke, A. D. "Rome and Italy." In D. W. J. Gill and C. Gempf, eds.,
The Book of Acts in Its Graeco-Roman Setting. Grand Rapids, MI:
Wm. B. Eerdmans, 1994.

Deissman, G. A. *Paul: A Study in Social and Religious History.*
London: Hodder and Stoughten, 1926.

Duncan, G. S. *Saint Paul's Ephesian Ministry.* London: Hodder and
Stoughten, 1929.

Dupont, J. *The Sources of Acts: The Present Position.* New York:
Herder and Herder, 1964.

Elderen, B.V. "Some Archeological Observations on Paul's First Missionary Journey." In W. W. Gasque and R. P. Martin, eds., *Apostolic History and the Gospel*. Grand Rapids, MI: Wm. B. Eerdmans, 1970.

Ellis, E. E. "Pastoral Letters." In G. F. Hawthorne, R. P. Martin, and D. G. Reid, eds., *Dictionary of Paul and His Letters*. Downers Grove, IL: InterVarsity Press, 1993.

Emmet, C. W. "The Case for the Tradition." In F. J. Foakes Jackson and K. Lake, eds., *Beginnings of Christianity*, Vol. II. London: MacMillan, 1922.

French, D. "Acts and the Roman Roads of Asia Minor." In D. W. J. Gill and C. Gempf, eds., *The Book of Acts in Its Graeco-Roman Setting*. Grand Rapids, MI: Wm. B. Eerdmans, 1994.

Gasque, W. W. *A History of the Interpretation of the Acts of the Apostles*. Peabody, MA: Hendrickson Publishers, 1989.

Gill, D. W. J. "Achaia." In D. W. J. Gill and C. Gempf, eds., *The Book of Acts in Its Graeco-Roman Setting*. Grand Rapids, MI: Wm. B. Eerdmans, 1994.

Gill, D. W. J. "Acts and the Urban Elites." In D. W. J. Gill and C. Gempf, eds., *The Book of Acts in Its Graeco-Roman Setting*. Grand Rapids, MI: Wm. B. Eerdmans, 1994.

Gutherie, D. *New Testament Introduction*. Downers Grove, IL: InterVarsity Press, 1970.

Hansen, G. W. "Galatia." In D. W. J. Gill and C. Gempf, eds., *The Book of Acts in Its Graeco-Roman Setting*. Grand Rapids, MI: Wm. B. Eerdmans, 1994.

Hanson, R. P. C. *The Acts*. Oxford: Clarendon, 1967.

Harnack, A. *The Acts of the Apostles*. New York: G. P. Putnam's, 1909

Harnack, A. *Luke the Physician*. New York: G. P. Putnam's, 1907.

Hemer, C. J. *The Book of Acts in the Setting of Hellenistic History*. Winona Lake, IN: Eisenbrauns, 1990.

Hengel, M. *Acts and the History of Earliest Christianity*. London: SCM, 1979.

Hengel, M. "The Geography of Palestine in Acts." In R. Bauckham, ed., *The Book of Acts in Its Palestinian Setting*. Grand Rapids, MI: Wm. B. Eerdmans, 1995.

Hock, R. F. *The Social Context of Paul's Ministry: Tentmaking and Apostleship*. Philadelpia: Fortress, 1980.

Horsely, G. H. R. "The Politarchs." In D. W. J. Gill and C. Gempf, eds., *The Book of Acts in Its Graeco-Roman Setting*. Grand Rapids, MI: Wm. B. Eerdmans, 1994.

Hughes, P. E. *Paul's Second Epistle to the Corinthians*. Grand Rapids, MI: Wm. B. Eerdmans, 1962.

Kearsly, R. A. "The Asiarchs." In D. W. J. Gill and C. Gempf, eds., *The Book of Acts in Its Graeco-Roman Setting*. Grand Rapids, MI: Wm. B. Eerdmans, 1994.

Lake, K. "Conversion of Paul and the Events Immediately Surrounding It." In K. Lake and H. J. Cadbury, eds., *The Beginnings of Christianity*, Vol. V. London: MacMillan, 1933.

Lake, K. *The Earlier Epistles of St. Paul*. London: Rivingtons, 1911.

Lake, K. and H. J. Cadbury, eds., *The Beginnings of Christianity*, Vol. IV. London: MacMillan, 1932.

Linnemann, E. *Historical Criticism of the Bible: Methodology or Ideology?* Grand Rapids: Baker Book House, 1990.

Longenecker, R. *Biblical Exegesis in the Apostolic Period*. Grand Rapids, MI: Wm. B. Eerdmans, 1975.

Longenecker, R. N. *Galatians*. Dallas, TX: Word, 1990.

Marshall, I. H. *The Acts of the Apostles*. Grand Rapids, MI: Wm. B. Eerdmans, 1980.

Marshall, I. H. "How Does One Write on the Theology of Acts?" In I. H. Marshall and D. Peterson, eds., *Witness to the Gospel: The Theology of Acts*. Grand Rapids, MI: Wm. B. Eerdmans, 1998.

Martin, R. P. *Philippians*. Grand Rapids, MI: Wm. B. Eerdmans, 1987.

Nobbs, A. "Cyprus." In D. W. J. Gill and C. Gempf, eds., *The Book of Acts in Its Graeco-Roman Setting*. Grand Rapids, MI: Wm. B. Eerdmans, 1994.

Ogilvie, R. M. "Phoenix." *Journal of Theological Studies*, 1958, pp. 308-314.

Paley, W. *Horae Paulinae*. Dublin: W. M'Kenzie, 1790.

Palmer, D. W. "Acts and the Ancient Historical Monograph." In B. Winter and A. D. Clarke, eds., *The Book of Acts in Its Ancient Literary Setting*. Grand Rapids, MI: Wm. B. Eerdmans, 1993.

Ramsay, W. M. *The Bearing of Recent Discovery On the Trustworthiness of the New Testament*. London: Hodder and Stoughten, 1915.

Ramsay, W. M. *Historical Commentary on St. Paul's Epistle to the Galatians*. New York: G. P. Putnam's, 1900.

Ramsay, W. M. *St. Paul the Traveller and Roman Citizen*. London: Hodder and Stoughten, 1897.

Rapske, B. "Acts, Travel, and Shipwreck." In D. W. J. Gill and C. Gempf, eds., *The Book of Acts in Its Graeco-Roman Setting*. Grand Rapids, MI: Wm. B. Eerdmans, 1994.

Rapske, B. *The Book of Acts and Paul in Roman Custody*. Grand Rapids, MI: Wm. B. Eerdmans, 1994.

Ridderbos, H. N. *The Epistle of Paul to the Churches of Galatia*. Grand Rapids, MI: Wm. B. Eerdmans, 1953.

Sherwin-White, A. N. *Roman Society and Roman Law in the New Testament*. Oxford: Clarendon, 1963.

Smith, J. *The Voyage and Shipwreck of St. Paul*. London: Longmans, Green, 1880.

Thompson, J. A. *The Bible and Archeology*. Grand Rapids, MI: Wm. B. Eerdmans, 1977.

Trebilco, P. "Asia." In D. W. J. Gill and C. Gempf, eds., *The Book of Acts In Its Graeco-Roman Setting*. Grand Rapids, MI: Wm. B. Eerdmans, 1994.

Trebilco, P. "Itineraries, Travel Plans, Journeys, Apostolic Parousia." In G. F. Hawthorne, R. P. Martin, and D. G. Reid, eds., *Dictionary of Paul and His Letters*. Downers Grove, IL: InterVarsity Press, 1993.

Winter, B. W. "The Imperial Cult." In D. W. J. Gill and C. Gempf, eds., *The Book of Acts in Its Graeco-Roman Setting*. Grand Rapids, MI: Wm. B. Eerdmans, 1994.

Winter, B. W. "Official Proceedings and the Forensic Speeches in Acts 24-26." In B. W. Winter and A. D. Clarke, eds., *The Book of Acts in Its Ancient Literary Setting*. Grand Rapids, MI: Wm. B. Eerdmans, 1993.

Witherington, B. *Grace in Galatia*. Grand Rapids, MI: Wm. B. Eerdmans, 1998.

Witherington, B. *Women in the Earliest Churches*. New York: Cambridge University Press, 1988.

Paul's Chronology

The chronology of Paul's life can only be a matter of approximate dating. Internally, Acts is often vague when it comes to relating matters of time. Externally, there are two sources that allow us to establish exact dates in relation to the events recorded in Acts. We know that the Emperor Claudius expelled the Jews from Rome around 50 AD, and also know that Gallio served as Proconsul of Corinth in 51 AD. These two events are also recorded in Acts and occurred during Paul's second journey. From these two dates we can reconstruct the following chronology:

Year (AD)	Event
30	Jesus' resurrection
33-35	Paul's conversion / sojourn in Damascus (Acts 9)
35	Paul's first post-conversion visit to Jerusalem
35-45	Paul's years in Cilicia, Syria and Antioch (Gal 1.21-2.1, Acts 9.30 / 11.25)

46	Paul's second post-conversion visit to Jerusalem (Acts 11.30)
47-48	The First Journey (Acts 13-14)
48	*Letter to the Galatians*
49	The Jerusalem Council (Acts 15)
49-52	The Second Journey (Acts 16-18)
50	*Letters to the Thessalonians*
52	Return visit to Jerusalem and Antioch
52-57	The Third Journey (Acts 18-21)
54	*First Letter to the Corinthians*
56	*Second Letter to the Corinthians*
57	*Letter to the Romans*
57-59	Paul's Judean arrest and trial (Acts 21-26)
59-60	Voyage to Rome and shipwreck (Acts 27-28)
60-62	House arrest in Rome and *Early Prison Letters*
62	Hearing before the Emperor and acquittal
62-64	Journey to Spain, Corinth, and Ephesus
65	Paul's re-arrest, *Later Prison Letters*, and execution in Rome

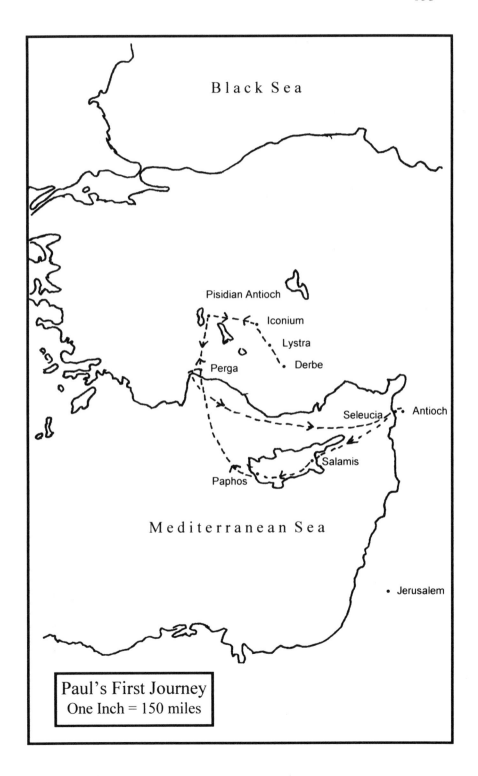

Black Sea

Pisidian Antioch

Iconium

Lystra

Derbe

Perga

Seleucia

Antioch

Salamis

Paphos

Mediterranean Sea

Jerusalem

Paul's First Journey
One Inch = 150 miles

154

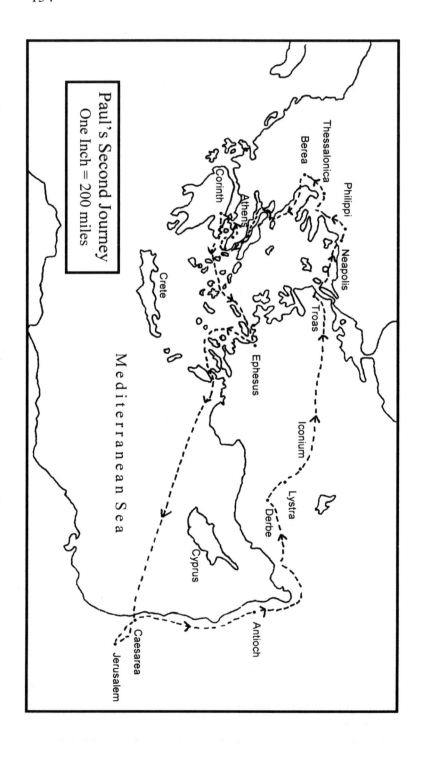

Paul's Second Journey
One Inch = 200 miles

Thessalonica
Berea
Philippi
Neapolis
Corinth
Athens
Troas
Crete
Ephesus
Iconium
Lystra
Derbe
Mediterranean Sea
Cyprus
Antioch
Caesarea
Jerusalem

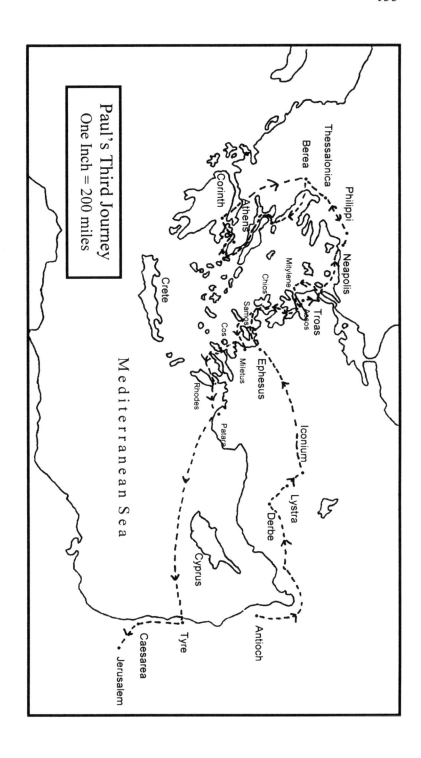

Paul's Third Journey
One Inch = 200 miles

Mediterranean Sea

Crete

Corinth

Athens

Berea

Thessalonica

Philippi

Neapolis

Mitylene

Chios

Samos

Assos

Troas

Cos

Miletus

Ephesus

Rhodes

Patara

Iconium

Lystra

Derbe

Cyprus

Antioch

Tyre

Caesarea

Jerusalem

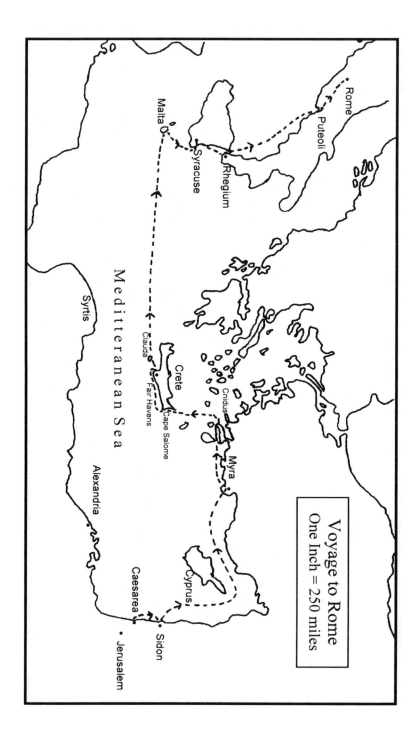

Voyage to Rome
One Inch = 250 miles

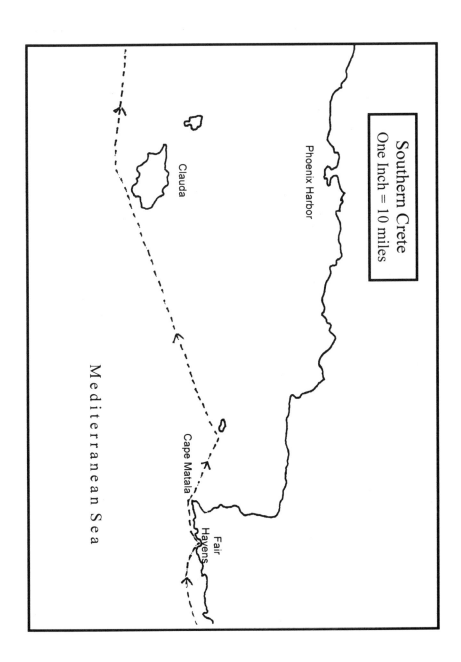

Southern Crete
One Inch = 10 miles

Phoenix Harbor

Clauda

Mediterranean Sea

Cape Matala

Fair
Havens

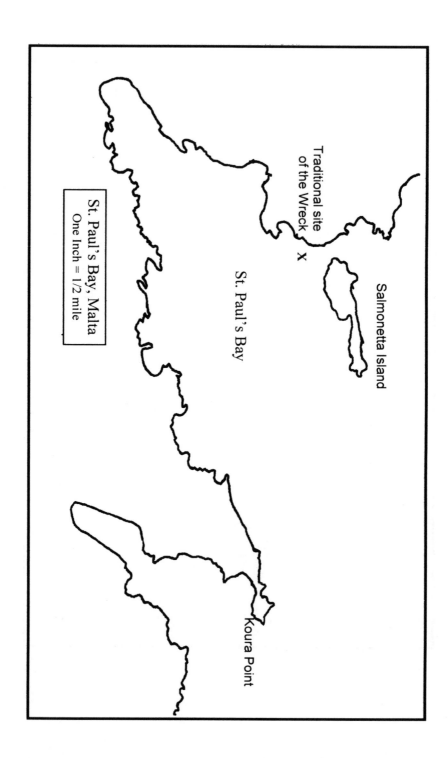

St. Paul's Bay, Malta
One Inch = 1/2 mile

St. Paul's Bay

Traditional site
of the Wreck   x

Salmonetta Island

Koura Point

Index

Evidence and Paul's Journeys

is the perfect gift for that thinking
relative or friend.

Every effort has been made to make it permanently available
online.

Buy it now at your favorite web bookstore
or go to:

www.parsagard.com
